The Emperor of the East by Philip Massinger

Philip Massinger was baptized at St. Thomas's in Salisbury on November 24th, 1583.

Massinger is described in his matriculation entry at St. Alban Hall, Oxford (1602), as the son of a gentleman. His father, who had also been educated there, was a member of parliament, and attached to the household of Henry Herbert, 2nd Earl of Pembroke. The Earl was later seen as a potential patron for Massinger.

He left Oxford in 1606 without a degree. His father had died in 1603, and accounts suggest that Massinger was left with no financial support this, together with rumours that he had converted to Catholicism, meant the next stage of his career needed to provide an income.

Massinger went to London to make his living as a dramatist, but he is only recorded as author some fifteen years later, when The Virgin Martyr (1621) is given as the work of Massinger and Thomas Dekker.

During those early years as a playwright he wrote for the Elizabethan stage entrepreneur, Philip Henslowe. It was a difficult existence. Poverty was always close and there was constant pleading for advance payments on forthcoming works merely to survive.

After Henslowe died in 1616 Massinger and John Fletcher began to write primarily for the King's Men and Massinger would write regularly for them until his death.

The tone of the dedications in later plays suggests evidence of his continued poverty. In the preface of The Maid of Honour (1632) he wrote, addressing Sir Francis Foljambe and Sir Thomas Bland: "I had not to this time subsisted, but that I was supported by your frequent courtesies and favours."

The prologue to The Guardian (1633) refers to two unsuccessful plays and two years of silence, when the author feared he had lost popular favour although, from the little evidence that survives, it also seems he had involved some of his plays with political characters which would have cast shadows upon England's alliances.

Philip Massinger died suddenly at his house near the Globe Theatre on March 17th, 1640. He was buried the next day in the churchyard of St. Saviour's, Southwark, on March 18th, 1640. In the entry in the parish register he is described as a "stranger," which, however, implies nothing more than that he belonged to another parish.

Index of Contents

DRAMATIS PERSONSAE

Theodosius the younger, the emperor
Paulinus, a kinsman to the emperor
Philanax, captain of the guard
Timantus   }
Chrysasius   } Eunuchs of the Emperor's chamber
Gratianus   }
Cleon, a traveller, friend to Paulinus
Patriarch
Informer
Projector
Master of the Habits and Manners
Minion of the Suburbs
Countryman
Surgeon
Empiric
Pulcheria, the protectress, sister to the emperor
Athenais, a strange Virgin, afterwards empress, and named Eudocia
Arcadia }
Flacilla } the younger sisters of the emperor
Officers, Suitors, Attendants, Guards, Huntsman, Executioners, Servants, &c.

PROLOGUE

AT THE BLACKFRIARS

But that imperious custom warrants it,
Our author with much willingness would omit
This preface to his new work. He hath found,
(And suffer d for t,) many are apt to wound
His credit in this kind: and, whether he
Express himsef fearful, or peremptory,
He cannot 'scape their censures who delight
To misapply whatever he shall write.
'Tis his hard fate. And though he will not sue,
Or basely beg such suffrages, yet, to you,
free and ingenious spirits, he doth now,
In me, present his service, with his vow,
He hath done his best: and, though he cannot glory
In his invention, (this work being a story
Of reverend antiquity,) he doth hope
In the proportion of it, and the scope,

You may observe some pieces drawn like one
Of a stedfast hand; and, with the whiter stone.
To be marked in your fair censures. More than
I am forbid to promise, and it is
With the most till you confirm it: since I've know
Whate' er the shaft be, archer, or the bow
From which 'tis sent, it cannot hit the white.
Unless your approbation guide it right.

PROLOGUE AT COURT

As ever, sir, you lent a gracious ear
To oppress' d innocence, now vouchsafe to hear
A short petition. At your feet, in me,
The poet kneels, and to your majesty
Appeals for justice. What we now present,
When first conceived, in his vote and intent,
Was sacred to your pleasure; in each part,
With his best of fancy, judgment, language, art,
Fashion d and form d so, as might well, and may
Deserve a welcome, and no vulgar way.
He durst not, sir, at such a solemn feast,
Lard his grave matter with one scurrilous jest;
But labour d that no passage might appear,
But what the queen without a blush might hear:
And yet this poor work suffered by the rage
And envy of some Catos of the stage:
Yet still he hopes this Play, which then was seen
With sore eyes, and condemn d out of their spleen,
May be by you, the supreme judge, set free,
And raised above the reach of calumny.

SCENE: Constantinople.

ACT I

SCENE I. A Room in the Palace

Enter **PAULINUS** and **CLEON**.

PAULINUS
In your six years' travel, friend, no

doubt, you have met with
Many and rare adventures, and observed
The wonders of each climate, varying in
The manners and the men; and so return,
For the future service of your prince and country,
In your understanding better'd.

CLEON
Sir, I have made of it
The best use in my power, and hope my gleanings
After the full crop others reap'd before me,
Shall not, when I am call'd on, altogether
Appear unprofitable: yet I left
The miracle of miracles in our age
At home behind me; every where abroad,
Fame, with a true though prodigal voice, deliver'd
Such wonders of Pulcheria, the princess,
To the amazement, nay, astonishment rather,
Of such as heard it, that I found not one,
In all the states and kingdoms that I pass'd through,
Worthy to be her second.

PAULINUS
She, indeed, is
A perfect phoenix, and disdains a rival.
Her infant years, as you know, promised much,
But, grown to ripeness, she transcends, and makes
Credulity her debtor. I will tell you,
In my blunt way, to entertain the time,
Until you have the happiness to see her,
How in your absence she hath borne herself,
And with all possible brevity; though the subject
Is such a spacious field, as would require
An abstract of the purest eloquence
(Derived from the most famous orators
The nurse of learning, Athens, shew'd the world)
In that man, that should undertake to be
Her true historian.

CLEON
In this you shall do me
A special favour.

PAULINUS
Since Arcadius' death,
Our late great master, the protection of
The prince, his son, the second Theodosius,
By a general vote and suffrage of the people,

Was to her charge assign'd, with the disposure
Of his so many kingdoms. For his person,
She hath so train'd him up in all those arts
That are both great and good, and to her wish'd
In an imperial monarch, that the mother
Of the Gracchi, grave Cornelia, Rome still boasts of,
The wise Pulcheria but named, must be
No more remember'd. She, by her example,
Hath made the court a kind of academy,
In which true honour is both learn'd and practised:
Her private lodgings a chaste nunnery,
In which her sisters, as probationers, hear
From her, their sovereign abbess, all the precepts
Read in the school of virtue.

CLEON
You amaze me.

PAULINUS
I shall, ere I conclude; for here the wonder
Begins, not ends. Her soul is so immense,
And her strong faculties so apprehensive,
To search into the depth of deep designs,
And of all natures, that the burthen, which
To many men were insupportable,
To her is but a gentle exercise,
Made, by the frequent use, familiar to her.

CLEON
With your good favour, let me interrupt you.
Being, as she is, in every part so perfect,
Methinks that all kings 'of our eastern world
Should become rivals for her.

PAULINUS
So they have;
But to no purpose. She, that knows her strength
To rule and govern monarchs, scorns to wear
On her free neck the servile yoke of marriage;
And for one loose desire, envy itself
Dares not presume to taint her. Venus' son
Is blind indeed when he but gazes on her;
Her chastity being a rock of diamonds,
With which encounter'd, his shafts fly in splinters;
His flaming torches in the living spring
Of her perfections quench'd: and, to crown
She's so impartial when she sits upon
The high tribunal, neither sway'd with pity,

Nor awed by fear, beyond her equal scale,
That 'tis not superstition to believe
Astrea once more lives upon the earth,
Pulcheria's breast her temple.

CLEON
You have given her
An admirable character.

PAULINUS
She deserves it:
And, such is the commanding power of virtue,
That from her vicious enemies it compels
Paeans of praise, as a due tribute to her.

[Loud music.

CLEON
What means this solemn music?

PAULINUS
Sir, it ushers
The emperor's morning meditation,
In which Pulcheria is more than assistant.
'Tis worth your observation, and you may
Collect from her expense of time this day,
How her hours, for many years, have been disposed of.

CLEON
I am all eyes and ears.

[After a strain of solemn music, **PHILANAX**, **TIMANTUS**, **PATRIARCH**, **THEODOSIUS**, **PULCHERIA**, **FLACCILLA**, and **ARCADIA**; followed by **CHRYSAPIUS** and **GRATIANUS**; **SERVANTS**, and **OFFICERS**.

PULCHERIA
Your patience, sir.
Let those corrupted ministers of the court,
Which you complain of, our devotions ended,
Be cited to appear: for the ambassadors
Who are importunate to have audience,
From me you may assure them, that tomorrow
They shall in public kiss the emperor's robe,
And we in private, with our soonest leisure,
Will give them hearing. Have you especial care too,
That free access be granted unto all
Petitioners. The morning wears. Pray you, on, sir;
Time lost is ne'er recover'd.

[Exeunt all but **PAULINUS** and **CLEON**.

PAULINUS
Did you note
The majesty she appears in?

CLEON
Yes, my good lord;
I was ravish'd with it.

PAULINUS
And then, with what speed
She orders her dispatches, not one daring
To interpose; the emperor himself,
Without reply, putting in act whatever
She pleased to impose upon him.

CLEON
Yet there were some,
That in their sullen looks, rather confess 'd
A forced constraint to serve her, than a will
To be at her devotion; what are they?

PAULINUS
Eunuchs of the emperor's chamber, that repine
The globe and awful sceptre should give place
Unto the distaff; for, as such, they whisper
A woman's government, but dare not yet
Express themselves.

CLEON
From whence are the ambassadors
To whom she promised audience?

PAULINUS
They are
Employ 'd by divers princes, who desire
Alliance with our emperor, whose years now,
As you see, write him man. One would advance
A daughter to the honour of his bed;
A second, his fair sister: to instruct you
In the particulars would ask longer time
Than my own designs give way to. I have letters
From special friends of mine, that to my care
Commend a stranger virgin, whom this morning
I purpose to present before the princess:
If you please, you may accompany me.

CLEON
I'll wait on you.

Exeunt.

SCENE II. Another Room in the Same

Enter the **INFORMER**, with **OFFICERS** bringing **PROJECTOR**, the **MINION of the SUBURBS**, and the **MASTER of the HABIT and MANNERS**.

INFORMER
Why should you droop, or hang your working heads?
No danger is meant to you; pray bear up:
For aught I know, you are cited to receive
Preferment due to your merits.

PROTECTOR
Very likely:
In all the projects I have read and practised,
I never found one man compell'd to come,
Before the seat of justice, under guard,
To receive honour.

INFORMER
No! it may be, you are
The first example. Men of qualities,
As I have deliver'd you to the protectress,
Who knows how to advance them, cannot conceive
A fitter place to have their virtues publish 'd,
Than in open court. Could you hope that the princess,
Knowing your precious merits, will reward them
In a private corner? No; you know not yet
How you may be exalted.

MINION
To the gallows.

INFORMER
Fie!
Nor yet depress'd to the galleys; in your names
You carry no such crimes: your specious titles
Cannot but take her: President of the Projectors!
What a noise it makes! The Master of the Habit!
How proud would some one country be that I know,
To be your first pupil! Minion of the Suburbs,
And now and then admitted to the court,

And honour 'd with the style of Squire of Dames!
What hurt is in it! One thing I must tell you,
As I am the state-scout, you may think me an informer.

MASTER
They are synonyma.

INFORMER
Conceal nothing from her
Of your good parts, 'twill be the better for you;
Or if you should, it matters not; she can conjure,
And I am her ubiquitary spirit,
Bound to obey her: you have my instructions;
Stand by, here's better company.

[Enter **PAULINUS, CLEON**, and. **ATHENAIS**, with a petition.

ATHENAIS
Can I hope, sir,
Oppressed innocence shall find protection
And justice among strangers, when my brothers,
Brothers of one womb, by one sire begotten,
Trample on my afflictions?

PAULINUS
Forget them,
Remembering those may help you.

ATHENAIS
They have robb'd me
Of all means to prefer my just complaint,
With any promising hope to gain a hearing,
Much less redress: petitions not sweetened
With gold, are but unsavory, oft refused;
Or, if received, are pocketed, not read.
A suitor's swelling tears, by the glowing beams
Of choleric authority are dried up
Before they fall, or, if seen, never pitied.
What will become of a forsaken maid!
My flattering hopes are too weak to encounter
With my strong enemy, despair, and 'tis
In vain to oppose her.

CLEON
Cheer her up; she faints, sir.

PAULINUS
This argues weakness; though, your brothers were

Cruel beyond expression, and the judges
That sentenced you, corrupt, you shall find; here
One of your own fair sex to do you right;
Whose beams of justice, like the sun, extend
Their light and heat to strangers, and are not!
Municipal or confined.

ATHENAIS
Pray you, do not feed me
With airy hopes: unless you can assure me
The great Puicheria will descend to hear
My miserable story, it were better
I died without the trouble.

PAULINUS
She is bound to it
By the surest chain, her natural inclination
To help the afflicted; nor shall long delays,
More terrible to miserable suitors
Than quick denials, grieve you. Dry your fair eyes.
This room will instantly be sanctified
With her bless'd presence; to her ready hand
Present your grievances, and rest assured
You. shall depart contented.

ATHENAIS
You breathe in me
A second life.

INFORMER
Will your lordship please to hear
Your servant a few words?

PAULINUS
Away, you rascal!
Did I ever keep such servants?

INFORMER
If your honesty
Would give you leave, it would be for your profit.

PAULINUS
To make use of an informer! tell me, in what
Can you advantage me?

INFORMER
In the first tender
Of a fresh suit never begg'd yet.

PAULINUS
What's your suit, sir?

INFORMER
Tis feasible: here are three arrant knaves
Discovered by my art.

PAULINUS
And thou the archknave:
The great devour the less.

INFORMER
And with good reason;
I must eat one a month, I cannot live else.

PAULINUS
A notable cannibal! but should I hear thee,
In what do your knaves concern me?

INFORMER
In the begging
Of their estates.

PAULINUS
Before they are condemn'd

INFORMER
Yes, or arraign'd: your lordship may speak too late else.
They are your own, and I will be content
With the fifth part of a share.

PAULINUS
Hence, rogue!

INFORMER
Such rogues
In this kind will be heard and cherish'd too.
Fool that I was, to offer such a bargain
To a spiced-conscience chapman! but I care not;
What he disdains to taste, others will swallow.

[Loud Music.

[Enter **THEODOSIUS, PULCHERIA, ARCADIA, FLACCILLA, PATRIARCH, PHILANAX, TIMANTHUS, CHRYSAPIUS, GRATIANUS,** and **ATTENDANTS.**

CLEON

They are return'd from the temple.

PAULINUS
See, she appears;
What think you now?

ATHENAIS
A cunning painter thus,
Her veil ta'en off, and awful sword and Pulcheria balance
Laid by, would picture Justice.

PULCHERIA
When you please,
You may intend those royal exercises
Suiting your birth and greatness: I will bear
The burthen of your cares, and, having purged
The body of your empire of ill humours,
Upon my knees surrender it.

CHRYSAPIUS
Will you ever
Be awed thus like a boy?

GRATIANUS
And kiss the rod
Of a proud mistress?

TIMANTUS
Be what you were born, sir.

PHILANAX
Obedience and majesty never lodged
In the same inn.

THEODOSIUS
No more; he never learn'd
The right way to command, that stopp'd his ears
To wise directions.

PULCHERIA
Read o'er the papers
I left upon my cabinet, two hours hence
I will examine you.

FLACCILLA
We spend our time well!
Nothing but praying and poring on a book.
It ill agrees with my constitution, sister.

Would I had been born some masquing-lady's woman,
Only to see strange sights, rather than live thus!

FLACCILLA
We are gone, forsooth; there is no remedy, sister.

[Exeunt **ARCADIA** and **FLACCILLA**.

GRATIANUS
What hath his eye found out?

TIMANTUS
'Tis fix'd upon
That stranger lady.

CHRYSAPIUS
I am glad yet, that
He dares look on a woman.

[All this time the **INFORMER** is kneeling to **PULCHERIA**, and delivering papers.

THEODOSIUS
Philanax,
What is that comely stranger?

PHILANAX
A petitioner.

CHRYSAPIUS
Will you hear her case, and dispatch her in your chamber?
I'll undertake to bring her.

THEODOSIUS
Bring me to
Some place where I may look on her demeanor:
'Tis a lovely creature!

CHRYSAPIUS
There's some hope in this yet.

[Flourish.

[Exeunt **THEODOSIUS, PATRIARCH, PHILANAX, TIMANTUS, CHRYSAPIUS,** and **GRATIANUS.**

PULCHERIA
No; you have done your parts.

PAULINUS

Now opportunity courts you,
Prefer your suit.

ATHENAIS [Kneeling]
As low as misery
Can fall, for proof of my humility,
A poor distressed virgin bows her head,
And lays hold on your goodness, the last altar
Calamity can fly to for protection.
Great minds erect their never-falling trophies
On the firm base of mercy; but to triumph
Over a suppliant, by proud fortune captived,
Argues a bastard conquest: 'tis to you
I speak, to you, the fair and just Pulcheria,
The wonder of the age, your sex's honour;
And as such, deign to hear me. As you have
A soul moulded from heaven, and do desire
To have it made a star there, make the means
Of your ascent to that celestial height
Virtue, wing'd with brave action: they draw near
The nature and the essence of the gods,
Who imitate their goodness.

PULCHERIA
If you were
A subject of the empire, which your habit
In every part denies

ATHENAIS
O, fly not to
Such an evasion! whate'er I am,
Being a woman, in humanity
You are bound to right me. Though the difference
Of my religion may seem to exclude me
From your defence, which you would have confined;
The moral virtue, which is general,
Must know no limits. By these blessed feet,
That pace the paths of equity, and tread boldly
On the stiff neck of tyrannous oppression,
By these tears by which I bathe them, I conjure you
With pity to look on me!

PULCHERIA
Pray you, rise;
And, as you rise, receive this comfort from me.
Beauty, set off with such sweet language, never
Can want an advocate; and you must bring
More than a guilty cause if you prevail not.

Some business, long since thought upon, dispatch'd,
You shall have hearing, and, as far as justice
Will warrant me, my best aids.

ATHENAIS
I do desire
No stronger guard; my equity needs no favour.

[Walks aside.

PULCHERIA
Are these the men?

PROJECTOR
We were, an't like your highness,
The men, the men of eminence and mark,
And may continue so, if it please your grace.

MASTER
This speech was well projected.

PULCHERIA
Does your conscience,
I will begin with you, whisper unto you
What here you stand accused of? Are you named
The President of Projectors?

INFORMER
Justify it, man,
And tell her in what thou'rt useful.

PROJECTOR
That is apparent;
And if you please, ask some about the court,
And they will tell you, to my rare inventions
They owe their bravery, perhaps means to purchase,
And cannot live without me. I, alas!
Lend out my labouring brains to use, and sometimes
For a drachma in the pound, the more the pity
I am all patience, and endure the curses
Of many, for the profit of one patron.

PULCHERIA
I do conceive the rest. What is the second?

INFORMER
The Minion of the Suburbs.

PULCHERIA
What hath he
To do in Constantinople?

MINION
I steal in now and then,
As I am thought useful; marry, there I am call'd
The Squire of Dames, or Servant of the Sex,
And by the allowance of some sportful ladies,
Honour 'd with that title.

PULCHERIA
Spare your character,
You are here decipher'd: stand by with your compeer.
What is the third? a creature I ne'er heard of:
The Master of the Manners and the Habit!
You have a double office.

MASTER
In my actions
I make both good; for by my theorems
Which your polite and terser gallants practise,
I re-refine the court, and civilize
Their barbarous natures. I have in a table,
With curious punctuality set down,
To a hair's breadth, how low a new-stamp'd courtier
May vail to a country gentleman, and by
Gradation, to his merchant, mercer, draper,
His linen-man, and tailor.

PULCHERIA
Pray you, discover,
This hidden mystery.

MASTER
If the foresaid courtier
(As it may chance sometimes) find not his name
Writ in the citizens' books, with a state hum
He may salute them after three days waiting;
But, if he owe them money, that he may
Preserve his credit, let him in policy never
Appoint a day of payment, so they may hope still:
But, if he be to take up more, his page
May attend them at the gate, and usher them
Into his cellar, and when they are warm'd with wine,
Conduct them to his bedchamber; and though then
He be under his barber's hands, as soon as seen,
He must start up to embrace them, vail thus low;

Nay, though he call them cousins, 'tis the better,
His dignity no way wrong'd in't.

PAULINUS
Here's a fine knave!

PULCHERIA
Does this rule hold without exception, sirrah,
For courtiers in general?

MASTER
No, dear madam,
For one of the last edition; and for him
I have composed a dictionary, in which
He is instructed, how, when, and to whom,
To be proud or humble; at what times of the year
He may do a good deed for itself, and that is
Writ in dominical letters; all days else
Are his own, and of those days the several hours
Mark'd out, and to what use.

PULCHERIA
Shew us your method;
I am strangely taken with it.

MASTER
'Twill deserve
A pension, I hope. First, a strong cullis
In his bed, to heighten appetite; shuttlecock,
To keep him in breath when he rises; tennis courts
Are chargeable, and the riding of great horses
Too boisterous for my young courtier: let the old ones
I think not of, use it; next, his meditation
How to court his mistress, and that he may seem witty,
Let him be furnish'd with confederate jests
Between him and his friend, that, on occasion,
They may vent them mutually: what his pace and garb
Must be in the presence, then the length of his sword,
The fashion of the hilt what the blade is
It matters not, 'twere barbarism to use it.
Unless to shewhis strength upon an andiron;
So, the sooner broke the better.

PULCHERIA
How I abuse
This precious time! Projector, I treat first
Of you and your disciples; you roar out,
All is the king's, his will above his laws;

And that fit tributes are too gentle yokes
For his poor subjects: whispering in his ear,
If he would have their fear, no man should dare
To bring a salad from his country garden.
Without the paying gabel; kill a' hen,
Without excise: and that if he desire
To have his children or his servants wear
Their heads upon their shoulders, you affirm
In policy 'tis fit the owner should
Pay for them by the poll; or, if the prince want
A present sum, he may command a city
Impossibilities, and for non-performance,
Compel it to submit to any fine
His officers shall impose. Is this the way
To make our emperor happy? can the groans
Of his subjects yield him music? must his thresholds
Be wash 'd with widows and wrong'd orphans' tears,
Or his power grow contemptible?

PROJECTOR
I begin
To feel myself a rogue again.

PULCHERIA
But you are
The squire of dames, devoted to the service
Of gamesome ladies, the hidden mystery
Discover 'd, their close bawd, thy slavish breath
Fanning the fires of lust; the go-between
This female and that wanton sir; your art
Can blind a jealous husband, and, disguised
Like a milliner or shoemaker, convey
A letter in a pantofle or glove,
Without suspicion, nay, at his table,
In a case of picktooths; you instruct them how
To parley with their eyes, and make the temple
A mart of looseness: to discover all
Your subtile brokages, were to teach in public
Those private practices which are, in justice,
Severely to be punish 'd.

MINION
I am cast:
A jury of my patronesses cannot quit me.

PULCHERIA
You are master of the manners and the habit;
Rather the scorn of such as would live men,

And not, like apes, with servile imitation
Study prodigious fashions. You keep
Intelligence abroad, that may instruct
Our giddy youth at home what new-found fashion
Is not in use, swearing he's most complete
That first turns monster. Know, villains,
I can thrust
This arm into your hearts, strip off the flesh;
That covers your deformities, and shew you
In your own nakedness. Now, though the: law
Call not your follies death, you are for ever
Banish'd my brother's court. Away with them;
I will hear no reply.

[Exeunt **INFORMER**, and **OFFICERS** with the **PROJECTOR**, **MINION of the SUBURBS**, and **MASTER of the HABIT and MANNERS**.

[**ATHENAIS** comes forward.

[Enter above, **THEODOSIUS**, **PHILANAX**, **TIMANTHUS**, **CHRYSAPIUS**, and **GRATIANUS**.

PAULINUS
What think you now?

CLEON
That I am in a dream; or that I see
A second Pallas.

PULCHERIA
These removed, to you
I clear my brow. Speak without fear, sweet maid,
Since, with a mild aspect, and ready ear
I sit prepared to hear you.
A then. Know, great princess,
My father, though a pagan, was admired
For his deep search into those hidden studies,
Whose knowledge is denied to common men:
The motion, with the divers operations
Of the superior bodies, by his long
And careful observation were made
Familiar to him; all the secret virtues
Of plants and simples, and in what degree
They were useful to mankind, he could discourse of:
In a word, conceive him as a prophet honour 'd
In his own country. But being born a man,
It lay not in him to defer the hour
Of his approaching death, though long foretold:
In this so fatal hour he call'd before him

His two sons and myself, the dearest pledges
Lent him by nature, and with his right hand
Blessing our several heads, he thus began.

CHRYSAPIUS
Mark his attention.

PHILANAX
Give me leave to mark too.

ATHENAIS
If I could leave my understanding to you
It were superfluous to make division.
Of whatsoever else I can bequeath you:
But, to avoid contention I allot
An equal portion of my possessions
To you, my sons; but unto thee, my daughter,
My joy, my darling, (pardon me, though I
Repeat his words,) if my prophetic soul,
Ready to take her flight, can truly guess at
Thy future fate, I leave the strange assurance
Of the greatness thou art born to, unto which
Thy brothers shall be proud to pay their service
Paulinus
And all men else, that honour beauty.

THEODOSIUS
Umph!

ATHENAIS
Yet to prepare thee for that certain fortune,
And that I may from present wants defend thee,
I leave ten thousand crowns: which said, being call'd
To the fellowship of our deities, he expired,
And with him all remembrance of the charge
Concerning me, left by him to my brothers.

PULCHERIA
Did they detain your legacy?

ATHENAIS
And still do.
His ashes were scarce quiet in his urn,
When, in derision of my future greatness,
They thrust me out of doors, denying me
One short night's harbour.

PULCHERIA

Weep not.

ATHENAIS
I desire,
By your persuasion, or commanding power,
The restitution of mine own; or that,
To keep my frailty from temptation,
In your compassion of me, you would please,
I, as an handmaid, may be entertain'd
To do the meanest offices to all such
As are honour'd in your service.

PULCHERIA
Thou art welcome.
What is thy name?

ATHENAIS
The forlorn Athenais.

PULCHERIA
The sweetness of thy innocence
strangely takes me.

[Takes her up and kisses her.

Forget thy brothers wrongs; for I will be
In my care a mother, in my love a sister to thee;
And, were it possible thou couldst be won
To be of our belief

PAULINUS
May it please your excellence,
That is an easy task; I, though no scholar,
Dare undertake it; clear truth cannot want
Rhetorical persuasions.

PULCHERIA
Tis a work,
My lord, will well become you. Break up the court:
May your endeavours prosper!

PAULINUS
Come, my fair one;
I hope, my convert.

ATHENAIS
Never: I will die
As I was born,

PAULINUS
Better you ne'er had been.

[Exeunt

PHILANAX
What does your majesty think of? the maid's gone.

THEODOSIUS
She's wondrous fair, and in her speech appear'd
Pieces of scholarship.

CHRYSAPIUS
Make use of her learning
And beauty together; on my life she will be proud
To be so converted.

THEODOSIUS
From foul lust heaven guard me!

ACT II

SCENE I. A Room in the Palace

Enter **PHILANAX, TIMANTUS, CHRYSAPIUS,** and **GRATIANUS.**

PHILANAX
We only talk, when we should do.

TIMANTUS
I'll second you;
Begin, and when you please.

GRATIANUS
Be constant in it.

CHRYSAPIUS
That resolution which grows cold to-day,
Will freeze to-morrow.

GRATIANUS
'Slight! I think she'll keep him
Her ward for ever, to herself engrossing
The disposition of all the favours
And bounties of the empire.

CHRYSAPIUS
We, that, by
The nearness of our service to his person,
Should raise this man, or pull down that without
Her license hardly dare prefer a suit,
Or if ye do, 'tis cross'd.

PHILANAX
You are troubled for
Your proper ends; my aims are high and honest,
The wrong that's done to majesty I repine at:
I love the emperor, and 'tis my ambition
To have him know himself, and to that purpose
I'll run the hazard of a check.

GRATIANUS
And I
The loss of my place.

TIMANTUS
I will not come behind,
Fall what can fall.

CHRYSAPIUS
Let us put on sad aspects,
To draw him on; charge home, we'll fetch you off,
Or lie dead by you.

[Enter **THEODOSIUS**.

THEODOSIUS
How's this? clouds in the chamber,
And the air clear abroad!

PHILANAX
When you, our sun,
Obscure your glorious beams, poor we that borrow
Our little light from you, cannot but suffer
A general eclipse.

TIMANTUS
Great sir, 'tis true;
For, till you please to know and be yourself,
And freely dare dispose of what's your own,
Without a warrant, we are falling' meteors,
And not fix'd stars.

CHRYSAPIUS
The pale-faced moon, that should
Govern the night, usurps the rule of day,
And still is at the full in spite of nature,
And will not know a change.

THEODOSIUS
Speak you in riddles?
I am no Œdipus, but your emperor,
And as such would be instructed.

PHILANAX
Your command
Shall be obey'd: till now, I never heard you
Speak like yourself; and may that Power, by which
You are so, strike me dead, if what I shall
Deliver as a faithful subject to you,
Hath root or growth from malice, or base envy
Of your sister's greatness! I could honour in her
A power subordinate to yours; but not,
As 'tis, predominant.

TIMANTUS
Is it fit that she,
In her birth your vassal, should command the knees
Of such as should not bow but to yourself?

GRATIANUS
She with security walks upon the heads
Of the nobility; the multitude,
As to a deity, offering sacrifice
For her grace and favour.

CHRYSAPIUS
Her proud feet even wearied
With the kisses of petitioners.

GRATIANUS
While you,
To whom alone such reverence is proper,
Pass unregarded by.

TIMANTUS
You have not yet,
Been master of one hour of your whole life.

CHRYSAPIUS
Your will and faculties kept in more awe

Than she can do her own.

PHILANAX
And as a bondman,
(O let my zeal find grace, and pardon from you,
That I descend so low,) you are design 'd
To this or that employment, suiting well
A private man, I grant, but not a prince.
To be a perfect horseman, or to know
The words of the chase, or a fair man of arms,
Or to be able to pierce to the depth,
Or write a comment on the obscurest poets,
I grant are ornaments; but your main scope
Should be to govern men, to guard your own,
If not enlarge your empire.

CHRYSAPIUS
You are built up
By the curious hand of nature, to revive
The memory of Alexander, or by
A prosperous success in your brave actions,
To rival Caesar.

TIMANTUS
Rouse yourself, and let not
Your pleasures be a copy of her will.

PHILANAX
Your pupilage is past, and manly actions
Are now expected from you.

GRATIANUS
Do not lose
Your subjects' hearts.

TIMANTUS
What is't to have the means
To be magnificent, and not exercise
The boundless virtue?

GRATIANUS
You confine yourself
To that which strict philosophy allows of,
As if you were a private man.

TIMANTUS
No pomp
Or glorious shows of royalty rendering it

Both loved and terrible.

GRATIANUS
Slight! you live, as it
Begets some doubt', whether you have, or not,
The abilities of a man.

CHRYSAPIUS
The firmament
Hath not more stars than there are several beauties
Ambitious, at the height, to impart their dear
And sweetest favours to you.

GRATIANUS
Yet you have not
Made choice of one, of all the sex, to serve you,
In a physical way of courtship.

THEODOSIUS
But that I would not
Begin the expression of my being a man,
In blood, or stain the first white robe I wear
Of absolute power, with a servile imitation
Of any tyrannous habit, my just anger
Prompts me to make you, in your sufferings, feel,
And not in words to instruct you, that the license
Of the loose and saucy language you now practised
Hath forfeited your heads.

GRATIANUS
How's this!

PHILANAX
I know not
What the play may prove, but I assure you that
I do not like the prologue.

THEODOSIUS
O the miserable
Condition of a prince; who, though he vary
More shapes than Proteus, in his mind and manners
He cannot win an universal suffrage
From the many-headed monster, multitude!
Like Æsop's foolish frogs, they trample on him
As a senseless block, if his government be easy;
And, if he prove a stork, they croak and rail
Against him as a tyrant. I will put off
That majesty, of which you think I have

Nor use nor feeling; and in arguing with you,
Convince you with strong proofs of common reason,
And not with absolute power, against which, wretches,
You are not to dispute. Dare you, that are
My creatures, by my prodigal favours fashion'd,
Presuming on the nearness of your service,
Set off with my familiar acceptance,
Condemn my obsequiousness to the wise directions
Of an incomparable sister, whom all parts
Of our world, that are made happy in the knowledge
Of her perfections, with wonder gaze on?
And yet you, that were only born to eat
The blessings of our mother earth, that are
Distant but one degree from beasts, (since slaves
Can claim no larger privilege,) that know
No further than your sensual appetites,
Or wanton lusts, have taught you, undertake
To give your sovereign laws to follow that
Your ignorance marks out to him!

[Walks by.

GRATIANUS
How were we
Abused in our opinion of his temper!

PHILANAX
We had forgot 'tis found in holy writ,
That kings' hearts are inscrutable.

TIMANTUS
I ne'er read it;
My study lies not that way.

PHILANAX
By his looks,
The tempest still increases.

THEODOSIUS
Am I grown
So stupid, in your judgments, that you dare,
With such security, offer violence
To sacred majesty? will you not know
The lion is a lion, though he shew not
His rending paws, or fill the affrighted air
With the thunder of his roarings? You bless'd saints,
How am I trenched on! Is that temperance
So famous in your cited Alexander,

Or Roman Scipio, a crime in me?
Cannot I be an emperor, unless
Your wives and daughters bow to my proud lusts?
And, 'cause I ravish not their fairest buildings
And fruitful vineyards, or what is dearest,
From such as are my vassals, must you conclude
I do not know the awful power and strength
Of my prerogative? Am I close-handed,
Because I scatter not among you that
I must not call mine own? know you, court leeches,
A prince is never so magnificent
As when he's sparing to enrich a few
With the injuries of many. Could your hopes
So grossly flatter you, as to believe
I was born and train'd up as an emperor, only
In my indulgence to give sanctuary,
In their unjust proceedings, to the rapine
And avarice of my grooms?

PHILANAX
In the true mirror
Of your perfections, at length we see
Our own deformities.

TIMANTUS
And not once daring
To look upon that majesty we now slighed

CHRYSAPIUS
With our faces thus glued to the earth, we beg
Your gracious pardon.

GRATIANUS
Offering our necks
To be trod on, as a punishment for our late
Presumption, and a willing testimony
Of our subjection.

THEODOSIUS
Deserve our mercy
In your better life hereafter; you shall find,
Though, in my father's life, I held it madness
To usurp his power, and in my youth disdain'd not
To learn from the instructions of my sister,
I'll make it good to all the world I am
An emperor; and even this instant grasp
The sceptre, my rich stock of majesty
Entire, no scruple wasted.

PHILANAX
If these tears
I drop proceed not from my joy to hear this,
May my eyeballs follow them!

TIMANTUS
I will shew myself,
By your sudden metamorphosis, transform'd
From what I was.

GRATIANUS
And ne'er presume to ask
What fits not you to give.

THEODOSIUS
Move in that sphere,
And my light with full beams shall shine upon you.
Forbear this slavish courtship, 'tis to me
In a kind idolatrous.

PHILANAX
Your gracious sister.

[Enter **PULCHERIA** and **SERVANT**.

PULCHERIA
Has he converted her?
Sen'. And, as such, will
Present her, when you please.

PULCHERIA
I am glad of it.
Command my dresser to adorn her with
The robes that I gave order for.

SERVANT
I shall.

PULCHERIA
And let those precious jewels T took last
Out of my cabinet, if 't be possible,
Give lustre to her beauties; and, that done,
Command her to be near us.

SERVANT
'Tis a province
I willingly embrace.

[Exit.

PULCHERIA
O my dear sir,
You have forgot your morning task, and therefore,
With a mother's love, I come to reprehend you;
But it shall be gently.

THEODOSIUS
'Twill become you, though
You said, with reverend duty. Know, hereafter,
If my mother lived in you, howe'er her son,
Like' you she were my subject.

PULCHERIA
How!

THEODOSIUS
Put off
Amazement; you will find it. Yet I'll hear you
At distance, as a sister, but no longer
As a governess, I assure you.

GRATIANUS
This is put home.

TIMANTUS
Beyond our hopes.

PHILANAX
She stands as if his words
Had powerful magic in them.

THEODOSIUS
Will you have me
Your pupil ever? the down on my chin
Confirms I am a man, a man of men,
The emperor, that knows his strength.

PULCHERIA
Heaven giant
You know it not too soon!

THEODOSIUS
Let it suffice
My wardship's out. If your design concerns us
As a man, and not a boy, with our allowance

You may deliver it.

PULCHERIA
A strange alteration!
But I will not contend. Be as you wish, sir,
Your own disposer; uncompell'd I cancel
All bonds of my authority.

[Kneels.

THEODOSIUS
You in this
Pay your due homage, which perform'd, I thus
Embrace you as a sister;

[Raises her.

No way doubting
Your vigilance for my safety as my honour;
And what you now come to impart, I rest
Most confident, points at one of them.

PULCHERIA
At both;
And not alone the present, but the future
Tranquillity of your mind; since in the choice
Of her you are to heat with holy fires,
And make the consort of your royal bed,
The certain means of glorious succession,
With the true happiness of our human being,
Are wholly comprehended.

THEODOSIUS
How! a wife?
Shall I become a votary to Hymen,
Before my youth hath sacrificed to Venus?
'Tis something with the soonest: yet, to shew,
In things indifferent, I am not averse
To your wise counsels, let me first survey
Those beauties, that, in being a prince, I know
Are rivals for me. You will not confine me
To your election; I must see, dear sister,
With mine own eyes.

PULCHERIA
'Tis fit, sir. Yet, in this,
You may please to consider, absolute princes
Have, or should have, in policy, less free will

Than such as are their vassals: for, you must,
As you are an emperor, in this high business
Weigh with due providence, with whom alliance
May be most useful for the preservation
Or increase of your empire.

THEODOSIUS
I approve not
Such compositions for our moral ends,
In what is in itself divine, nay, more,
Decreed in heaven. Yet, if our neighbour princes,
Ambitious of such nearness, shall present
Their dearest pledges to me, (ever reserving
The caution of mine own content,) I will not
Contemn their courteous offers.

PULCHERIA
Bring in the pictures.

[Two pictures brought in.

THEODOSIUS
Must I then judge the substances by the shadows?
The painters are most envious, if they want
Good colours for preferment: virtuous ladies
Love this way to be flattered, and accuse
The workman of detraction, if he add not
Some grace they cannot truly call their own.
Is't not so, Gratianus? you may challenge
Some interest in the science.

GRATIANUS
A pretender
To the art, I truly honour, and subscribe
To your majesty's opinion.

THEODOSIUS
Let me see
[Reads.
Cleanthe, daughter to the king of Epire,
Ætatis suæ, the fourteenth: ripe enough,
And forward too, I assure you. Let me examine
The symmetries. If statuaries could
By the foot of Hercules set down punctually
His whole dimensions, and the countenance be
The index of the mind, this may instruct me,
With the aids of that I've read touching this subject,
What she is inward. The colour of her hair,

If it be, as this does promise, pale and faint,
And not a glistering white; her brow, so so;
The circles of her sight, too much contracted;
Juno's fair cow-eyes by old Homer are
Commended to their merit: here's a sharp frost,
In the tip of her nose, which, by the length, assures me
Of storms at midnight, if I fail to pay her
The tribute she expects. I like her not:
What is the other?

CHRYSAPIUS
How hath he commenced
Doctor in this so sweet and secret art,
Without our knowledge?

TIMANTUS
Some of his forward pages
Have robbed us of the honour.

PHILANAX
No such matter;
He has the theory only, not the practic.

THEODOSIUS [reads]
Amasia, sister to the duke of Athens;
Her age eighteen, descended lineally
from Theseus, as by her pedigree
Will be made apparent. Of his lusty kindred,
And lose so much time! 'tis strange! as I live, she hath
A philosophical aspect; there is
More wit than beauty in her face; and when
I court her, it must be in tropes, and figures,
Or she will cry, Absurd! she will have her elenchs
To cut off any fallacy I can hope
To put upon her, and expect I should
Ever conclude in syllogisms, and those true ones
In parte et toto: or she'll tire me with
Her tedious elocutions in the praise of
The increase of generation, for which
Alone, the sport, in her morality,
Is good and lawful, and to be often practised
For fear of missing. Fie on't! let the race
Of Theseus be match'd with Aristotle's:
I'll none of her.

PULCHERIA
You are curious in your choice, sir,
And hard to please; yet, if that your consent

May give authority to it, I'll present you
With one, that, if her birth and fortunes answer
The rarities of her body and her mind,
Detraction durst not tax her.

THEODOSIUS
Let me see her,
Though wanting those additions, which we can
Supply from our own store: it is in us
To make men rich and noble; but to give
Legitimate shapes and virtues does belong
To the great Creator of them, to whose bounties
Alone 'tis proper, and in this disdains
An emperor for his rival.

PULCHERIA
I applaud
This fit acknowledgment; since princes then
Grow less than common men, when they contend
With him, by whom they are so.

[Enter **PAULINUS**, **CLEON**, and **ATHENAIS**, richly habited.

THEODOSIUS
I confess it.

PULCHERIA
Not to hold you in suspense, behold the virgin,
Rich in her natural beauties, no way borrowing
The adulterate aids of art. Peruse her better;
She's worth your serious view.

PHILANAX
I am amazed too:
I never saw her equal.

GRATIANUS
How his eye
Is fix'd upon her!

TIMANTUS
And, as she were a fort
He'd suddenly surprise, he measures her
From the bases to the battlements.

CHRYSAPIUS
Ha! now I view her better,
I know her; 'tis the maid that not long since

Was a petitioner; her bravery
So alters her, I had forgot her face.

PHILANAX
So has the emperor.

PAULINUS
She holds out yet,
And yields not to the assault.

CLEON
She's strongly guarded
In her virgin blushes.

PAULINUS
When you know, fair creature,
It is the emperor that honours you
With such a strict survey of your sweet parts,
In thankfulness you cannot but return
Due reverence for the favour.
A then. I was lost
In my astonishment at the glorious object,
And yet rest doubtful whether he expects,
Being more than man, my adoration,
Since sure there is divinity about him:
Or will rest satisfied, if my humble knees
In duty thus bow to -him.

THEODOSIUS
Ha! it speaks.

PULCHERIA
She is no statue, sir.

THEODOSIUS
Suppose her one,
And that she had nor organs, voice, nor heat,
Most willingly I would resign my empire,
So it might.be to aftertimes recorded
That I was her Pygmalion; though, like him,
I doted on my workmanship, without hope too
Of having Cytherea so propitious
To my vows or sacrifice, in her compassion
To give it life or motion.

PULCHERIA
Pray you, be not rapt so,
Nor borrow from imaginary fiction

Impossible aids: she's flesh and blood, I assure you;
And if you please to honour her in the trial,
And be your own security, as you'll find
I fable not, she comes in a noble way
To be at your devotion.

CHRYSAPIUS
'Tis the maid
I offer'd to your highness; her changed shape
Conceal'd her from you.

THEODOSIUS
At the first I knew her,
And a second firebrand Cupid brings, to kindle
My flames almost put out: I am too cold,
And play with opportunity. May I taste then
The nectar of her lip?

[Kisses her.

I do not give it
The praise it merits: antiquity is too poor
To help me with a simile to express her:
Let me drink often from this living spring,
To nourish new- invention.

PULCHERIA
Do not surfeit
In over-greedily devouring that
Which may without satiety feast you often.
From the moderation in receiving them,
The choicest viands do continue pleasing
To the most curious palates. If you think her
Worth your embraces, and the sovereign title
Of the Grecian Empress

THEODOSIUS
If! how much you sin,
Only to doubt it; the possession of her
Makes all that was before most precious to me,
Common and cheap: in this you've shewn yourself
A provident protectress. I already
Grow weary of the absolute command
Of my so numerous subjects, and desire
No sovereignty but here, and write down gladly
A period to my wishes.

PULCHERIA

Yet, before
It be too late, consider her condition;
Her father was a pagan, she herself
A new-converted Christian.

THEODOSIUS
Let me know
The man to whose religious means I owe
So great a debt.

PAULINUS
You are advanced too high, sir,
To acknowledge a beholdingness; 'tis discharged,
And I beyond my hopes rewarded, if
My service please your majesty.

THEODOSIUS
Take this pledge
Of our assured love. Are there none here
Have suits to prefer! on such a day as this
My bounty's without limit. O my dearest!
I will not hear thee speak; whatever in
Thy thoughts is apprehended, I grant freely:
Thou wouldst plead thy unworthiness. By thyself,
The magazine of felicity, in thy lowness
Our eastern queens, at their full height, bow to thee,
And are, in their best trim, thy foils and shadows!
Excuse the violence of my love, which cannot
Admit the least delay. Command the patriarch
With speed to do his holy office for us,
That, when we are made one

PULCHERIA
You must forbear, sir;
She is not yet baptized.

THEODOSIUS
In the same hour
In which she is confirmed in our faith,
We mutually will give away each other,
And both be gainers; we'll hear no reply
That may divert us. On.

PULCHERIA
You may hereafter
Please to remember to whose furtherance
You owe this height of happiness.
A then. As I was

Your creature when I first petition 'd you,
I will continue so, and you shall find me,
Though an empress, still your servant.

[All go off, but **PHILANAX**, **GRATIANUS**, and **TIMANTUS**.

GRATIANUS
Here's a marriage
Made up o' the sudden!

PHILANAX
I repine not at
The fair maid's fortune, though I fear the princess
Had some peculiar end in't.

TIMANTUS
Who's so simple
Only to doubt it?

GRATIANUS
It is too apparent;
She hath preferr'd a creature of her own,
By whose means she may still keep to herself
The government of the empire.

TIMANTUS
Whereas, if
The emperor had espoused some neighbour queen,
Pulcheria, with all her wisdom, could not
Keep her pre-eminence.

PHILANAX
Be it as it will,
'Tis not now to be alter'd. Heaven, I say,
Turn all to the best!

GRATIANUS
Are we come to praying again?

PHILANAX
Leave thy profaneness.

GRATIANUS
Would it would leave me!
I am sure I thrive not by it.

TIMANTUS
Come to the temple.

GRATIANUS
Even where you will I know not
what to think on't.

[Exeunt.

ACT III

SCENE I. A Room in the Palace

Enter **PAULINUS** and **PHILANAX**.

PAULINUS
Nor this, nor the age before us, ever look'd on
The like solemnity.

PHILANAX
A sudden fever
Kept me at home. Pray you, my lord, acquaint me
With the particulars.

PAULINUS
You may presume
No pomp nor ceremony could be wanting,
Where there was privilege to command, and means
To cherish rare inventions.

PHILANAX
I believe it;
But the sum of ail in brief.

PAULINUS
Pray you, so take it:
Fair Athenais, not long since a suitor,
And almost in her hopes forsaken, first
Was christen'd and the emperor's mother's name,
Eudocia, as he will'd, imposed upon her:
Pulcheria, the ever-matchless princess,
Assisted by her reverend aunt Maria,
Her godmothers.

PHILANAX
And who the masculine witness?

PAULINUS

At the new empress' suit, I had the honour;
For which I must ever serve her.

PHILANAX
'Twas a grace
With justice you may boast of.

PAULINUS
The marriage follow'd;
And, as 'tis said, the emperor made bold
To turn the day to night; for to bed they went
As soon as they had dined, and there are wagers
Laid by some merry lords, he hath already
Begot a boy upon her.

PHILANAX
That is yet
To be determined of; but I am certain
A prince, so soon in his disposition alter'd,
Was never heard nor read of.

PAULINUS
But of late,
Frugal and sparing, now nor bounds nor limits
To his magnificent bounties. He affirm'd
Having received more blessings by his empress
Than he could hope, in thankfulness to heaven
He cannot be too prodigal to others.
Whatever's offer'd to his royal hand,
He signs without perusing it.

PHILANAX
I am here
Enjoin'd to free all such as lie for debt,
The creditors to be paid out of his coffers.

PAULINUS
And I all malefactors that are not
Convicted or for treason or foul murder:
Such only are excepted.

PHILANAX
'Tis a rare clemency!

PAULINUS
Which we must not dispute, but put-
in practice.

[Exeunt.

SCENE II. Another Room in the Same

Loud Music

SHOUTS [within]
Heaven preserve the Emperor! Heaven bless the Empress!

Then enter in state, the **PATRIARCH, CHRYSAPIUS, PAULINUS, THEODOSIUS, EUDOCIA, PULCHERIA,
ARCADIA** and **FLACCILLA**, bearing Eudocia's train; followed by **PHILANAX, GRATIANUS**, and **TIMANTUS**.
Several **SUITORS** present petitions to the **EMPEROR**, which he seals.

PULCHERIA
Sir, by your own rules of philosophy,
You know things violent last not. Royal bounties
Are great and gracious, while they are dispensed
With moderation; but, when their excess
In giving giant-bulks to others, takes from
The prince's just proportion, they lose
The name of virtues, and, their natures changed,
Grow the most dangerous vices.

THEODOSIUS
In this, sister,
Your wisdom is not circular; they that sow
In narrow bounds, cannot expect in reason
A crop beyond their ventures: what I do
Disperse, I lend, and will with usury
Return unto my heap. I only then
Am rich and happy (though my coffers sound
With emptiness) when my glad subjects feel
Their plenty and felicity is my gift;
And they will find, when they with cheerfulness
Supply not my defects, I being the stomach
To the politic body of the state, the limbs
row suddenly faint and feeble: I could.
Proofs of more fineness in their shape and language,
But none of greater strength. Dissuade me not;
What we will, we will do; yet, to assure you
Your care does not offend us, for an hour
Pie happy in the converse of my best
And dearest comfort. May you please to license
My privacy some few minutes?

EUDOCIA

License, sir!
I have no will but is derived from yours,
And that still waits upon you; nor can I
Be left with such security with any
As with the gracious princess, who receives
Addition, though she be all excellence,
In being styled your sister.

THEODOSIUS
O sweet creature!
Let me be censured fond, and too indulgent,
Nay, though they say uxorious, I care not:
Her love and sweet humility exact
A tribute far above my power to pay
Her matchless goodness. Forward.

[Flourish.

[Exeunt all but **PULCHERIA**, **EUDOCIA**, **ARCADIA**, and **FLACCILLA**.

PULCHERIA
Now you find
Your dying father's prophecy, that foretold
Your present greatness, to the full accomplish'd,
For the poor aids and furtherance I lent you,
I willingly forget.

EUDOCIA
Even that binds me
To a more strict remembrance of the favour;
Nor shall you, from my foul ingratitude,
In any circumstance, ever find cause
To upbraid me with your benefit.

PULCHERIA
I believe so.
Pray you, give us leave:

[**ARCADIA** and **FLACCILLA** walk aside.

What now I must deliver
Under the deepest seal of secrecy,
Though it be for your good, will give assurance
Of what is look'd for, if you not alone
Hear, but obey my counsels.

EUDOCIA
They must be

Of a strange nature, if with zealous speed
I put them not in practice.

PULCHERIA
'Twere impertinence
To dwell on circumstances, since the wound
Requires a sudden cure; especially
Since you, that are the happy instrument
Elected to it, though young, in your judgment
Write far above your years, and may instruct
Such as are more experienced.

EUDOCIA
Good madam,
In this I must oppose you; I am well
Acquainted with my weakness, and it will not;
Become your wisdom, by which I am raised
To this titulary height, that should correct
The pride and overweening of my fortune,
To play the parasite to it, in ascribing
That merit to me, unto which I can
Pretend no interest: pray you, excuse
My bold simplicity, and to my weight
Design me where 'you please, 'and you shall find,
In my obedience, I am still your creature.

PULCHERIA
'Tis nobly answer'd, and I glory in
The building I have raised: go on, sweet lady,
In this your virtuous progress: but to the point.
You know, nor do I envy it, you have
Acquired that power which, not long since, was mine,
In governing the emperor, and must use
The strength you hold in the heart of his affections,
For his private, as the public preservation,
To which there is no greater enemy
Than his exorbitant prodigality,
Howe'er his sycophants and flatterers call it
Royal magnificence; and though you may
Urge what's done for your honour must not be
Curb'd or controll'd by you, you cannot in
Your wisdom but conceive, if that the torrent
Of his violent bounties be not stopp'd or lessen 'd,
It will prove most pernicious. Therefore, madam,
Since 'tis your duty, as you are his wife,
To give him saving counsels, and in being
Almost his idol, may command him to
Take any shape you please, with a powerful hand

To stop him in his precipice to ruin

EUDOCIA
Avert it, heaven!

PULCHERIA
Heaven is most gracious to you,
In choosing you to be the instrument
Of such a pious work. You see he signs
What suit soever is preferr'd, not once
Enquiring what it is, yielding himself
A prey to all; I would, therefore, have you, lady,
As I know you will, to advise him, or command him,
As he would reap the plenty of your favours,
To use more moderation in his bounties;
And that, before he gives, he would consider
The what, to whom, and wherefore.

EUDOCIA
Do you think
Such arrogance, or usurpation rather,
Of what is proper and peculiar
To every private husband, and much more
To him, an emperor, can rank with the obedience
And duty of a wife? Are we appointed
In our creation (let me reason with you)
To rule, or to obey? or, 'cause he loves me
With a kind impotence, must I tyrannize
Over his weakness, or abuse the strength
With which he arms me, to his wrong? or, like
A prostituted creature, merchandize
Our mutual delight for hire, or to
Serve mine own sordid 'ends? In vulgar nuptials
Priority is exploded, though there be
A difference in the parties; and shall I,
His vassal, from obscurity raised by him
To this so eminent light, presume t' appoint him
To do, or not to do, this, or that? When wives
Are well accommodated by their husbands,
With all things both for use and ornament,
Let them fix there, and never dare to question
Their wills or actions; for myself, I vow,
Though now my lord would rashly give away
His sceptre and imperial diadem,
Or if there could be anything more precious,
I would not cross it: but I know this is
But a trial of my temper, and as such
I do receive it; or, if 't be otherwise,

You are so subtle in your arguments,
I dare not stay to hear them.

[Offers to retire.

PULCHERIA
Is it even so?
I have power o'er these yet, and command their stay,
To harken nearer to me.

ARCADIA
We are charged
By the emperor, our brother, to attend
The empress' service.

FLACCILLA
You are too mortified, sister,
I (With reverence I speak it,) for young ladies,
To keep you company. I am so tired
With your tedious exhortations, doctrines, uses,
Of your religious morality,
That, for my health's sake, I must take the freedom
To enjoy a little of those pretty pleasures
That I was born to.

ARCADIA
When I come to your years,
I'll do as you do; but, till then, with your pardon,
I'll lose no more time. I have not learn'd to dance yet,
Nor sing, but holy hymns, and those to vile tunes too;
Nor to discourse, but of schoolmen's opinions.
How shall I answer my suitors, since, I hope,
Ere long I shall have many, without practice
To write, and speak, something that's not derived
From the fathers of philosophy?

FLACCILLA
We shall shame
Our breeding, sister, if we should go on thus.

ARCADIA
'Tis for your credit that we study
How to converse with men; women with women
Yields but a barren argument.

FLACCILLA
She frowns
But you'll protect us, madam?

EUDOCIA
Yes, and love
Your sweet simplicity.

ARCADIA
All young girls are so,
Till they know the way of it.

FLACCILLA
But, when we are enter 'd,
We shall on a good round pace.

EUDOCIA
I'll leave you, madam.

ARCADIA
And we our duties with you.

[Exeunt **EUDOCIA**, **ARCADIA**, and **FLACCILLA**.

PULCHERIA
On all hands
Thus slighted! no way left? Am I grown stupid
In my invention? can I make no use
Of the emperor's bounties? Now 'tis thought: within, there!

[Enter an **ATTENDANT**.

ATTENDANT
Madam.

PULCHERIA
It shall be so: nearer; your ear.
Draw a petition to this end.

[Whispers him.

ATTENDANT
Besides
The danger to prefer it, I believe
'Twill ne'er be granted.

PULCHERIA
How's this! are you grown,
From a servant, my director? let me hear
No more of this. Dispatch;

[Exit **ATTENDANT**.

I'll master him
At his own weapon.

[Enter **THEODOSIUS, PAULINUS, PHILANAX, TIMANTUS**, and **GRATIANUS**.

THEODOSIUS
Let me understand it,
If yet there be aught wanting that may perfect
A general happiness.

PAULINUS
The people's joys
In seas of acclamations flow in,
To wait on yours.

PHILANAX
Their love, with bounty levied,
Is a sure guard: obedience iorced from fear,
Paper fortification, which, in danger,
Will yield to the impression of a reed,
Or of itself fall off.

THEODOSIUS
True, Philanax;
And by that certain compass we resolve
To steer our bark of government.

[Re-enter **ATTENDANT** with the petition, which he secretly delivers to **PULCHERIA**.

PULCHERIA
'Tis well.

[Kneels.

THEODOSIUS
My dearest and my all-deserving sister
As a petitioner kneel! It must not be.
Pray you, rise; although your suit were half my empire,
Tis freely granted.

PULCHERIA
Your alacrity
To give hath made a beggar; yet, before
My suit is by your sacred hand and seal
Confirm'd, 'tis necessary you peruse
The sum of my request.

[Presents the petition.

THEODOSIUS
We will not wrong
Your judgment in conceiving what 'tis fit
For you to ask, and us to grant, so much,
As to proceed with caution; give me my signet:
With confidence I sign it, and here vow
By my father's soul, but with your free consent,
It is irrevocable.

TIMANTUS
What if she now,
Calling to memory how often we
Have crossed her government, in revenge hath made
Petition for our heads?

GRATIANUS
They must even off then;
No ransome can redeem us.

THEODOSIUS
Let those jewels
So highly rated by the Persian merchants,
Be bought, and as a sacrifice from us,
Presented to Eudocia, she being only
Worthy to wear them. I am angry with
The unresistible necessity
Of my occasions and important cares,
That so long keep me from her.

[Exeunt **THEODOSIUS, PAULINUS, PHILANAX, TIMANTUS,** and **GRATIANUS.**

PULCHERIA
Go to the empress,
And tell her, on the sudden I am sick,
And do desire the comfort of a visit,
If she please to vouchsafe it. From me use
Your humblest language

[Exit **ATTENDANT.**

—but, when once I have her
In my possession, I will rise and speak
In a higher strain: say it raise storms, no matter;
Fools judge by the event, my ends are honest.

[Exit.

Enter **THEODOSIUS, TIMANTUS, PHILANAX**.

THEODOSIUS
What is become of her? Can she, that carries
Such glorious excellence of light about her,
Be any where conceal'd?

PHILANAX
We have sought her lodgings,
And all we can learn from the servants, is
She, by your majesty's sisters waited on,
The attendance of her other officers,
By her express command, denied

THEODOSIUS
Forbear
Impertinent circumstances, whither went she? speak.

PHILANAX
As they guess, to the laurel grove.

THEODOSIUS
So slightly guarded!
What an earthquake I feel in me! and, but that
Religion assures the contrary,
The poets' dreams of lustful fauns and satyrs-
Would make me fear I know not what.

[Enter **PAULINUS**.

PAULINUS
I have found her,
An it please your majesty.

THEODOSIUS
Yes, it doth please me:
But why return'd without her?

PAULINUS
As she made
Her speediest approaches to your presence,
A servant of the princess's, Pulcheria,

Encounter'd her: what 'twas he whisper'd to her
I am ignorant; but hearing it, she started,
And will'd me to excuse her absence from you
The third part of an hour.

THEODOSIUS
In this she takes
So much of my life from me: yet, I'll bear it
With what patience I may, since 'tis her pleasure.
Go back, my good Paulinus, and entreat her
Not to exceed a minute.

TIMANTUS
Here's strange fondness!

[Exeunt.

SCENE IV. Another Room in the Same

Enter **PULCHERIA** and **SERVANTS**.

PULCHERIA
You are certain she will come?

SERVANT
She is already
Enter'd your outward lodgings.

PULCHERIA
No train with her?

SERVANT
Your excellence' sisters only.

PULCHERIA
'Tis the better.
See the doors strongly guarded, and deny
Access to all, but with our special license:
Why dost thou stay? shew your obedience,
Your wisdom now is useless.

[Exeunt **SERVANTS**,

[Enter **EUDOCIA**, **ARCADIA**, and **FLACCILLA**.

FLACCILLA

She is sick, sure,
Or, in fit reverence to your majesty,
She had waited you at the door.

ARCADIA
'Twould hardly be

[**PULCHERIA** walking by.

Excused, in civil manners, to her equal:
But with more difficulty to you, that are
So far above her.

EUDOCIA
Not in her opinion;
She hath been too long accustom'd to command,
To acknowledge a superior.

ARCADIA
There she walks.

FLACCILLA
If she be not sick of the sullens, I see not
The least infirmity in her.

EUDOCIA
This is strange!

ARCADIA
Open your eyes; the empress.

PULCHERIA
Reach that chair:
Now, sitting thus at distance, I'll vouchsafe
To look upon her.

ARCADIA
How, sister! pray you, awake;
Are you in your wits?

FLACCILLA
Grant, heaven, your too much learning
Does not conclude in madness!

EUDOCIA
You entreated
A visit from me.

PULCHERIA
True, my servant used
Such language; but now, as a mistress, I
Command your service.

EUDOCIA
Service!

ARCADIA
She's stark mad, sure.

PULCHERIA
You'll find I can dispose of what's mine own,
Without a guardian.

EUDOCIA
Follow me. I will see you
When your frantic fit is o'er. I do begin
To be of your belief.

PULCHERIA
It will deceive you.
Thou shalt not stir from hence: thus, as mine own,
I seize upon thee.

FLACCILLA
Help, help! violence
Offer'd to the empress' person!

PULCHERIA
'Tis in vain:
She was an empress once, but, by my gift;
Which being abused, I do recall my grant.
You are read in story; call to your remembrance
What the great Hector's mother, Hecuba,
Was to Ulysses, Ilium sack'd.

EUDOCIA
A slave.

PULCHERIA
To me thou art so.

EUDOCIA
Wonder and amazement
Quite overwhelm me: how am I transform'd?
How have I lost my liberty?

[Knocking within.

PULCHERIA
Thou shalt know
Too soon, no doubt.

[Enter a **SERVANT**.

Who's that, that with such rudeness
Beats at the door?

SERVANT
The prince Paulinus, madam;
Sent from the emperor, to attend upon
The gracious empress.

ARCADIA
And who is your slave now?

FLACCILLA
Sister, repent in time, and beg a pardon
For your presumption.

PULCHERIA
It is resolved:
From me return this answer to Paulinus,
She shall not come; she's mine; the emperor hath
No interest in her.

[Exit **SERVANT**,

EUDOCIA
Whatsoe'er I am,
You take not from your power o'er me, to yield
A reason for this usage.

PULCHERIA
Though my will is
Sufficient, to add to thy affliction,
Know, wretched thing, 'tis not thy fate, but folly,
Hath made thee what thou art: 'tis some delight
To urge my merits to one so ungrateful;
Therefore with horror hear it. When thou wert
Thrust, as a stranger, from thy father's house,
Exposed to all calamities that want
Could throw upon thee, thine own brothers' scorn,
And in thy hopes, as by the world, forsaken,
My pity the last altar that was left thee,

I heard thy syren charms, with feeling heard them,
And my compassion made mine eyes vie tears
With thine, dissembling crocodile! and when queens
Were emulous for thy imperial bed,
The garments of thy sorrows cast aside,
I put thee in a shape as would have forced
Envy from Cleopatra, had she seen thee.
Then, when I knew my brother's blood was warm'd
With youthful fires, I brought thee to his presence;
And how my deep designs, for thy good plotted,
Succeeded to my wishes, is apparent,
And needs no repetition.

EUDOCIA

I am conscious
Of your so many and unequall'd favours;
But find not how I may accuse myself
For any facts committed, that, with justice,
Can raise your anger to this height against me.

PULCHERIA

Pride and forgetfulness would not let thee see that,
Against which now thou canst not close thy eyes.
What injury could be equal to thy late
Contempt of my good counsel? When I urged
The emperor's prodigal bounties, and entreated
That you would use your power to give them limits,
Or, at the least, a due consideration
Of such as sued, and for what, ere he sign'd it;
In opposition, you brought against me
The obedience of a wife, that ladies were not,
Being well accommodated by their lords,
To question, but much less to cross, their pleasures;
Nor would you, though the emperor were resolved
To give away his sceptre, hinder it,
Since 'twas done for your honour; covering, with
False colours of humility, your ambition,

EUDOCIA

And is this my offence?

PULCHERIA

As wicked counsel
Is still most hurtful unto those that give it;
Such as deny to follow what is good,
In reason, are the first that must repent it.
When I please, you shall hear more; in the mean time,
Thank your own wilful folly, that hath changed you

From an empress to a bondwoman.

THEODOSIUS [within]
Force the doors;
Kill those that dare resist.

[Enter **THEODOSIUS**, **PAULINUS**, **PHILANAX**, **CHRYSAPIUS**, and **GRATIANUS**.

EUDOCIA
Dear sir, redeem me.

FLACCILLA
O suffer not, for your own honour's sake,
The empress, you so late loved, to be made
A prisoner in the court.

ARCADIA
Leap to his lips,
You'll find them the best sanctuary.

FLACCILLA
And try then,
What interest my reverend sister hath
To force you from them.

THEODOSIUS
What strange May-game's this?
Though done in sport, how ill this levity
Becomes your wisdom?

PULCHERIA
I am serious, sir,
And have done nothing but what you in honour,
And as you are yourself an emperor,
Stand bound to justify.

THEODOSIUS
Take heed; put not these
Strange trials on my patience.

PULCHERIA
Do not you, sir,
Deny your own act: As you are a man,
And stand on your own bottom, 'twill appear
A childish weakness to make void a grant
Sign'd by your sacred hand and seal, and strengthen'd
With a religious oath, but with my license
Never to be recall'd. For some few minutes

Let reason rule your passion, and in this

[Delivers the deed.

Be pleased to read my interest: you will find there,
What you in me call violence, is justice,
And that I may make use of what's my own,
According to my will. 'Tis your own gift, sir;
And what an emperor gives, should stand as firm
As the celestial poles upon the shoulders
Of Atlas, or his successor in that office,
The great Alcides.
Theo, Miseries of more weight
Than 'tis feign'd they supported, fall upon me.
What hath my rashness done! In this transaction,
Drawn in express and formal terms, I have
Given and consign'd into your hands, to use
And observe as you please, my dear Eudocia!
It is my deed, I do confess it is,
And, as I am myself, not to be cancell'd:
But yet you may shew mercy and you will,
When you consider that there is no beauty
So perfect in a creature, but is soil'd
With some unbeseeming blemish. You have labour'd
To build me up a complete prince, 'tis granted;
Yet, as I am a man, like other monarchs
I have defects and frailties: my facility
To send petitioners with pleased looks from me,
Is all I can be charged with; and it will
Become your wisdom,
(since 'tis in your power,)
In charity to provide I fall no further
Or in my oath, or honour.

PULCHERIA
Royal sir,
This was the mark I aim'd at, and I glory
At the length, you so conceive it: 'twas' a weakness
To measure, by your own integrity,
The purposes of others. I have shewn you,
In a true mirror, what fruit grows upon
The tree of hoodwink'd bounty, and what dangers
Precipitation, in the managing
Your great affairs, produceth.
Theo, I embrace it
As a grave advertisement, and vow hereafter
Never to sign petitions at this rate.

PULCHERIA
For mine, see, sir, 'tis cancell'd; on my knees
I re-deliver what I now begg'd from you.

[Tears the deed.

She is my second gift.

THEODOSIUS
Which if I part from
Till death divorce us

[Kisses **EUDOCIA**.

EUDOCIA
So, sir!

THEODOSIUS
Nay, sweet, chide not,
I am punish 'd in thy looks; defer the rest,
Till we are more private.

PULCHERIA
I ask pardon too,
If, in my personated passion, I
Appear'd too harsh and rough.

EUDOCIA
'Twas gentle language,
What I was then consider'd.

PULCHERIA
O, dear madam,
It was decorum in the scene.

EUDOCIA
This trial,
When I was Athenais, might have pass'd,
But as I am the empress

THEODOSIUS
Nay, no anger,
Since all good was intended.

[Exit **THEODOSIUS, EUDOCIA, ARCADIA**, and **FLACCILLA**.

PULCHERIA
Building on

That certain base, I fear not what can follow.

[Exit.

PAULINUS
These are strange devices, Philanax.

PHILANAX
True, my lord.
May all turn to the best!

GRATIANUS
The emperor's looks
Promised a calm.

CHRYSAPIUS
But the vex'd empress' frowns
Presaged a second storm.

PAULINUS
I am sure I feel one
In my leg already.

PHILANAX
Your old friend, the gout?

PAULINUS
My forced companion, Philanax.

CHRYSAPIUS
To your rest.

PAULINUS
Rest, and forbearing wine, with a temperate diet,
Though many mountebanks pretend the cure
I have found my best physicians.

PHILANAX
Ease to your lordship.

[Exeunt.

ACT IV

SCENE I. A Room in the Palace

Enter **EUDOCIA** and **CHRYSAPIUS**.

EUDOCIA
Make me her property!

CHRYSAPIUS
Your majesty
Hath just cause of distaste; and your resentment
Of the affront, in the point of honour, cannot
But meet a fair construction.

EUDOCIA
I have only
The title of an empress, but the power
Is by her ravish'd from me: she surveys
My actions as a governess, and calls
My not observing all that she directs,
Folly and disobedience.

CHRYSAPIUS
Under correction,
With grief I've long observed it; and, if you
Stand pleased to sign my warrant, I'll deliver,
In my unfeign'd zeal and desire to serve you,
(Howe'er I run the hazard of my head for't,
Should it arrive at the knowledge of the princess,)
Not alone the reasons why things are thus carried,
But give into your hands the power to clip
The wings of her command.

EUDOCIA
Your service this way
Cannot offend me.

CHRYSAPIUS
Be you pleased to know, then,
But still with pardon, if I am too bold.
Your too much sufferance imps the broken feathers
Which carry her to this proud height, in which
She with security soars, and still towers o'er you:
But if you would employ the strengths you hold
In the emperor's affections, and remember
The orb you move in should admit no star else,
You never would confess the managing
Of state affairs to her alone are proper,
And you sit by, a looker on.

EUDOCIA

I would not,
If it were possible I could attempt
Her diminution, without a taint
Of foul ingratitude in myself.

CHRYSAPIUS
In this
The sweetness of your temper does abuse you;
And you call that a benefit to yourself,
Which she, for her own ends, conferr'd upon you.
'Tis yielded, she gave way to your advancement:
But for what cause? that she might still continue
Her absolute sway and swing o'er the whole state:
And that she might to her admirers vaunt,
The empress was her creature, and the giver
To be preferr'd before the gift.

EUDOCIA
It may be.

CHRYSAPIUS
Nay, 'tis most certain: whereas would you please
In a true glass to look upon yourself,
And view, without detraction, your own merits,
Which all men wonder at, you would find that fate,
Without a second cause, appointed you
To the supremest honour. For the princess,
She hath reign'd long enough, and her remove
Will make your entrance free to the possession
Of what you were born to; and, but once resolve
To build upon her ruins, leave the engines
That must be used to undermine her greatness
To my provision.

EUDOCIA
I thank your care:
But a design of such weight must not be
Rashly determined of; it will exact
A long and serious consultation from me.
In the meantime, Chrysapius, rest assured
I live your thankful mistress. \Exit.

CHRYSAPIUS
Is this all?
Will the physic that I minister' d work no further?
I have play'd the fool; and, leaving a calm port,
Embark'd myself on a rough sea of danger,
in her silence lies my safety, which how can I

Hope from a woman? but the die is thrown,
And I must stand the hazard.

[Exit.

SCENE II. A Space before the Palace

Enter **THEODOSIUS, PHILANAX, TIMANTUS, GRATIANUS,** and **HUNTSMEN.**

THEODOSIUS
Is Paulinus
So tortured with his gout?

PHILANAX
Most miserably.
And it adds much to his affliction, that
The pain denies him power to wait upon
Your majesty.

THEODOSIUS
I pity him: he is
A wondrous honest man, and what he suffers,
I know, will grieve my empress.

TIMANTUS
He, indeed, is
Much bound to her gracious favour.

THEODOSIUS
He deserves it;
She cannot find a subject upon whom
She better may confer it.—Is the stag safe lodged?

GRATIANUS
Yes, sir, and the hounds and huntsmen ready.

PHILANAX
He will make you royal sport. He is a deer
Of ten, at the least.

[Enter a **COUNTRYMAN** with an apple.

GRATIANUS
Whither will this clown?

TIMANTUS

Stand back.

COUNTRYMAN
I would zee the emperor; why should you courtiers
Scorn a poor countryman? we zweat at the plough
To vill your mouths, you and your curs might starve else:
We prune the orchards, and you cranch the: fruit;
Yet still you're snarling at us.

THEODOSIUS
What's the matter?

COUNTRYMAN
I would look on thy zweet face,

TIMANTUS
Unmannerly swain!

COUNTRYMAN
Zwain! though I am a zwain, I! have a heart yet,
As ready to do service for my liege,
As any princox peacock of you all.
Zookers! had I one of you zingle, with this twig
I would soo veeze you.

TIMANTUS
Will your'majesty
Hear his rude language?

THEODOSIUS
Yes, and hold it as
An ornament, not a blemish. O, Timantus,
Since that dread Power by whom we are, disdains not
With an open ear to hear petitions from us; j
Easy access in us, his deputies,
To the meanest of our subjects, is a debt
Which we stand bound to pay.

COUNTRYMAN
By my granam's ghost
'Tis a holesome zaying! our vicar could not mend it
In the pulpit on a Zunday.

THEODOSIUS
What's thy suit.'friend?

COUNTRYMAN
Zute! I would laugh at that. Let the court beg from thee,

What the poor country gives: I bring a present
To thy good grace, which I can call mine own,
And look not, like these gay volk, fona return
Of what they venture. Have I giv'n't you? ha!

CHRYSAPIUS
A perilous knave.

COUNTRYMAN
Zee here a dainty apple,

[Presents the apple.

Of mine own grafting; zweet and zound, I assure thee.

THEODOSIUS
It is the fairest fruit I ever saw.
Those golden apples in the Hesperian orchards,
So strangely guarded by the watchful dragon
As they required great Hercules to get them;
Or those with which Hippomenes deceived
Swift-footed Atalanta, when I look
On this, deserve no wonder. You behold
The poor man and his present with contempt;
I to their value prize both: he that could
So aid weak nature by his care and labour,
As to compel a crab-tree stock to bear
A precious fruit of this large size and beauty,
Would by his industry change a petty village
Into a populous city, and from that
Erect a flourishing kingdom. Give the fellow,
For an encouragement to his future labours,
Ten Attic talents.

COUNTRYMAN
I will weary heaven
With my prayers for your majesty.

[Exit.

THEODOSIUS
Philanax,
From me present this rarity to the rarest
And best of women: when I think upon
The boundless happiness that from her flows to me,
In my imagination I am rapt
Beyond myself: but I forget our hunting.
To the forest, for the exercise of my body;

But for my mind, 'tis wholly taken up
In the contemplation of her matchless virtues.

[Exeunt.

SCENE III. A Room in the Palace

Enter **EUDOCIA**, **PULCHERIA**, **ARCADIA**, and **FLACCILLA**.

EUDOCIA
You shall know there's a difference between us.

PULCHERIA
There was, I am certain, not long since, when you
Kneel'd a petitioner to me; then you were happy
To be near my feet; and do you hold it now,
As a disparagement, that I side you, lady?

EUDOCIA
Since you respect me only as I was,
What I am shall be remember 'd.

PULCHERIA
Does the means
I practised, to give good and saving counsels
To the emperor, and your new-stamp'd majesty,
Still stick in your stomach?

EUDOCIA
'Tis not yet digested,
In troth it is not. Why, good governess,
Though you are held for a grand madam, and yourself
The first that overprize it, I ne'er took
Your words for Delphian oracles, nor your actions
For such wonders as you make them: there is one,
When she shall see her time, as fit and able
To be made partner of the emperor's cares,
As your wise self, and may with justice challenge
A nearer interest. You have done your visit,
So, when you please, you may leave me.

PULCHERIA
I'll not bandy
Words with your mightiness, proud one only this,
You carry too much sail for your small bark,
And that, when you least think upon't, may sink you.

[Exit.

FLACCILLA
I am glad she's gone.

ARCADIA
I fear'd she would have read
A tedious lecture to us.

[Enter **PHILANAX** with the apple.

PHILANAX
From the emperor,
This rare fruit to the rarest.

EUDOCIA
How, my lord!

PHILANAX
I use his language, madam; and that trust,
Which he imposed on me, discharged, his pleasure
Commands my present service.

[Exit.

EUDOCIA
Have you seen
So fair an apple!

FLACCILLA
Never.

ARCADIA
If the taste
Answer the beauty.

EUDOCIA
Prettily begg'd: you should have it,
But that you eat too much cold fruit, and that
Changes the fresh red in your cheeks to paleness.

[Enter a **SERVANT**.

I have other dainties for you: You come from
Paulinus; how is't with that truly noble,
And honest lord, my witness at the fount,
In a word, the man to whose bless'd charity

I owe my greatness? How is't with him?

SERVANT
Sprightly
In his mind; but, by the raging of his gout,
In his body much distemper'd; that you pleased
To inquire his health, took off much from his pain,
His glad looks did confirm it.

EUDOCIA
Do his doctors
Give him no hope?

SERVANT
Little; they rather fear
By his continual burning, that he stands
In danger of a fever.

EUDOCIA
To him again,
And tell him that I heartily wish it lay
In me to ease him; and from me deliver
This choice fruit to him; you may say to that,
I hope it will prove physical.

SERVANT
The good lord
Will be o'erjoyed with the favour.

EUDOCIA
He deserves more.

[Exeunt.

SCENE IV. A Room in Paulinus' House

PAULINUS discovered in a Chair, attended by a **SURGEON**.

SURGEON
I have done as much as art can do, to stop
The violent course of your fit, and I hope you feel it:
How does your honour?

PAULINUS
At some ease, I thank you;
I would you could assure continuance of it,

For the moiety of my fortune.

SURGEON
If I could cure
The gout, my lord, without the philosopher's stone
I should soon purchase, it being a disease
In poor men very rare, and in the rich
The cure impossible. Your many bounties
Bid me prepare you for a certain truth,
And to flatter you were dishonest.

PAULINUS
Your plain dealing
Deserves a fee. Would there were many more such
Of your profession! Happy are poor men!
If sick with the excess of heat or cold,
Caused by necessitous labour, not loose surfeits,
They, when spare diet, or kind nature fail
To perfect their recovery, soon arrive at
Their rest in death: but, on the contrary,
The great and noble are exposed as preys
To the rapine of physicians; and they,
In lingering out what is remediless,
Aim at their profit, not the patient's health.
A thousand trials and experiments
Have been put upon me, and I forced to pay dear
For my vexation; but I am resolved
(I thank your honest freedom) to be made
A property no more for knaves to work on.

[Enter **CLEON** with a parchment roll.

What have you there?

CLEON
The triumphs of an artsman
O'er all infirmities, made authentical
With the names of princes, kings, and emperors,
That were his patients.

PAULINUS
Some empiric.

CLEON
It may be so; but he swears, within three days
He'll grub up your gout by the roots, and make you able
To march ten leagues a day in complete armour.

PAULINUS
Impossible.

CLEON
Or, if you like not him

SURGEON
Hear him, my lord, for your mirth;
I will take order
They shall not wrong you.

PAULINUS
Usher in your monster.

CLEON
He is at hand. March up: now speak for yourself.

[Enter **EMPIRIC**.

EMPIRIC
I come not, right honourable, to your presence, with any base and sordid end of reward; the immortality of my fame is the white I shoot at: the charge of my most curious and costly ingredients frayed, amounting to some seventeen thousand crowns a trifle in respect of health writing your noble name in my catalogue, I shall acknowledge myself amply satisfied.

SURGEON
I believe so.

EMPIRIC
For your own sake, I most heartily wish that you had now all the diseases, maladies, and infirmities upon you, that were ever remembered by old Galen, Hippocrates, or the later and more admired Paracelsus.

PAULINUS
For your good wish, I thank you!

EMPIRIC
Take me with you, I beseech your good lordship. I urged it, that your joy, in being certainly and suddenly freed from them, may be the greater, and my not-to-be-paralleled skill the more remarkable. The cure of the gout a toy, without boast be it said, my cradle-practice: The cancer, the fistula, the dropsy, consumption of lungs and kidneys, hurts in the brain, heart, or liver, are things worthy my opposition; but in the recovery of my patients I ever overcome them. But to your gout

PAULINUS
Ay, marry, sir, that cured, I shall be apter
To give credit to the rest.

EMPIRIC
Suppose it done, sir.

SURGEON
And the means you use, I beseech you?

EMPIRIC
I will do it in the plainest language, and discover my ingredients. First, my boteni terebinthina of Cypris, my manna, ros ccelo, coagulated with vetulos ovorum, vulgarly yolks of eggs, with a little cyath or quantity of my potable elixir, with some few scruples of sassafras and guiacum, so taken every morning and evening, in the space of three days purgeth, cleanseth, and dissipateth the inward causes of the virulent tumour.

PAULINUS
Why do you smile?

SURGEON
When he hath done I will resolve you.

EMPIRIC
For my exterior applications, I have these balsum-unguentulums, extracted from herbs, plants, roots, seeds, gums, and a million of other vegetables, the principal of which are, Ulissipona, or serpentaria, sophia, or herba consolidarum, parthcnium, or com- manilla Romana, mumia transmarina, mixed with my plumbum philosophorum, and mater mctallorum, cum ossa paraleli, est uniziersalc medicamentum in podagra.

CLEON
A conjuring balsamum!

EMPIRIC
This applied warm upon the pained place, with a feather of struthio-cameli, or a bird of paradise, which is everywhere to be had, shall expulse this tartarous, viscous, anatheos, and malignant dolor.

SURGEON
An excellent receipt! but does your lordship
Know what 'tis good for?

PAULINUS
I would be instructed.

SURGEON
For the gonorrhoea, or, if you will; hear it
In a plainer phrase, the pox.

EMPIRIC
If it cure his lordship
Of that by the way, I hope, sir, 'tis the better.
My medicine serves for all things, and the pox, sir,
Though falsely named the sciatica, or gout,
Is the more catholic sickness.

PAULINUS
Hence with the rascal!
Yet hurt him not, he makes me smile, and that
Frees him from punishment.

[They thrust him off.

SURGEON
Such slaves as this
Render our art contemptible.

[Enter **SERVANT** with the apple.

SERVANT
My good lord.

PAULINUS
So soon return'd!

SERVANT
And with this present from
Your great and gracious mistress, with her wishes
It may prove physical to you.

PAULINUS
In my heart
I kneel, and thank her bounty.
Dear friend
Cleon,
Give him the cupboard of plate in the next room,
For a reward.

[Exeunt **CLEON** and **SERVANT**.

Most glorious fruit! but made
More precious by her grace and love that sent it:
To touch it only, coming from her hand,
Makes me forget all pain. A diamond
Of this large size, (though it would buy a kingdom,)
Hewed from the rock, and laid down at my feet,
Nay, though a monarch's gift, will hold no value,
Compared with this and yet, ere I presume
To taste it, though, sans question, it is
Some heavenly restorative, I in duty
Stand bound to weigh my own unworthiness.
Ambrosia is food only for the gods,
And not by human lips to be profaned.

Without a word concerning this, command
Eudocia to come to me.

[Exit **TIMANTUS**.

Would I had
Ne'er known her by that name, my mother's name,
Or that, for her own sake, she had continued
Poor Athenais still! No intermission!
Wilt thou so soon torment me? must I read,
Writ in the table of my memory,
To warrant my suspicion, how Paulinus
(Though ever thought a man averse to women)
First gave her entertainment, made her way
For audience to my sister? then I did
Myself observe how he was ravish 'd with
The gracious delivery of her story,
Which was, I grant, the bait that first took me, too:
She was his convert; what the rhetoric was
He used, I know not; and, since she was mine,
In private as in public what a mass
Of grace and favour hath she heap'd upon him!
And, but to-day, this fatal fruit She's come.

[Re-enter **TIMANTHUS** with **EUDOCIA**, **FLACCILLA**, and **ARCADIA**.

Can she be guilty?

EUDOCIA
You seem troubled, sir;
My innocence makes me bold to ask the cause,
That I may ease you of it. No salute,
After four long hours' absence!

THEODOSIUS
Prithee, forgive me.

[Kisses her.

Methinks I find Paulinus on her lips,
And the fresh nectar that I drew from thence
Is on the sudden pall'd. How have you spent
Your hours since I last saw you?

EUDOCIA
In the converse
Of your sweet sisters.

THEODOSIUS
Did not Philanax,
From me deliver you an apple?

EUDOCIA
Yes, sir;
Heaven, how you frown! pray you, talk of something else,
Think not of such a trifle.

THEODOSIUS
How, a trifle!
Does any toy from me presented to you,
Deserve to be so slighted? do you value
What's sent, and not the sender? from a peasant
It had deserved your thanks.

EUDOCIA
And meets from you, sir,
All possible respect.

THEODOSIUS
I prized it, lady,
At a higher rate than you believe; and would not
Have parted with it, but to one I did
Prefer before myself.

EUDOCIA
It was, indeed,
The fairest that I ever saw.

THEODOSIUS
It was;
And it had virtues in it, my Eudocia,
Not visible to the eye.

EUDOCIA
It may be so, sir.

THEODOSIUS
What did you with it? tell me punctually;
I look for a strict accompt.

EUDOCIA
What shall I answer? [Aside.

THEODOSIUS
Do you stagger? Ha!

EUDOCIA
No, sir; I have eaten it.
! It had the pleasant 'st taste! I wonder that
You found it not in my breath.

THEODOSIUS
I'faith, I did not,
And it was wonderous strange.

EUDOCIA
Pray you, try again.

THEODOSIUS
I find no scent oft here: you play with me;
You have it still?

EUDOCIA
By your sacred life and fortune,
An oath I dare not break, I have eaten it.

THEODOSIUS
Do you know how this oath binds?

EUDOCIA
Too well, to break it.

THEODOSIUS
That ever man, to please his brutish sense,
Should slave his understanding to his passions,
And, taken with soon-fading white and red,
Deliver up his credulous ears to hear
The magic of a Syren; and from these
Believe there ever was, is, or can be,
More than a seeming honesty in bad woman!

EUDOCIA
This is strange language.

THEODOSIUS
Who waits? Come all.

[Re-enter **PULCHERIA**, **PHILANAX**, **CHRYSAPIUS**, **GRATIANUS**, and **GUARD**.

Nay, sister, not so near, being of the sex,
I fear you are infected too.

PULCHERIA
What mean you?

THEODOSIUS

To shew you a miracle, a prodigy
Which Afric never equall'd: Can you think
This masterpiece of heaven, this precious vellum,
Of such a purity and virgin whiteness,
Could be design'd to have perjury and whoredom,
In capital letters, writ upon't?

PULCHERIA

Dear sir.

THEODOSIUS

Nay, add to this, an impudence beyond
All prostituted boldness. Art not dead yet?
Will not the tempests in thy conscience rend thee
As small as atoms, that there may no sign
Be left thou ever wert so? wilt thou live
Till thou art blasted with the dreadful lightning
Of pregnant and unanswerable proofs
Of thy adulterous twines? die yet, that I
With my honour may conceal it.

EUDOCIA

Would long since
The Gorgon of your rage had turn'd me marble!
Or, if I have offended

THEODOSIUS

If! good angels!
But I am tame; look on this dumb accuser.

[Shewing the apple.

EUDOCIA

Oh, I am lost!

THEODOSIUS

Did ever cormorant
Swallow his prey, and then digest it whole,
As she hath done this apple? Philanax,
As 'tis, from me presented it; the good lady
Swore she had eaten it; yet, I know not how,
It came entire into Paulinus' hands,
And I from him received it, sent in scorn,
Upon my life, to give me a close touch
That he was weary of thee. Was there nothing
Left thee to fee him to give satisfaction

I may adore it as some holy relic
Derived from thence, but impious to keep it
In my possession; the emperor only
Is worthy to enjoy it.

[Re-enter **CLEON**.

Go, good Cleon,
And (cease this admiration at this object,)
From me present this to my royal master,
I know it will amaze him; and excuse me
That I am not myself the bearer of it.
That I should be lame now, when with wings of duty
I should fly -to the service of this empress!
Nay, no delays, good Cleon.

CLEON
I am gone, sir.

[Exeunt.

SCENE V. A Room in the Palace

Enter **THEODOSIUS**, **CHRYSAPIUS**, **TIMANTUS**, and **GRATIANUS**.

CHRYSAPIUS
Are you not tired, sir?

THEODOSIUS
Tired! I must not say so,
However, though I rode hard. To a hunts man,
His toil is his delight, and to complain
Of weariness, would shew as poorly in him
As if a general should grieve for a wound
Received upon his forehead, or his breast,
After a glorious victory. Lay by
These accoutrements for the chase.

[Enter **PULCHERIA**.

PULCHERIA
You are well return'd, sir,
From your princely exercise.

THEODOSIUS
Sister, to you

I owe the freedom, and the use of all
The pleasures I enjoy: your care provides
For my security, and the burthen, which
I should alone sustain, you undergo,
And, by your painful watchings, yield my sleeps
Both sound and sure. How happy am I in
Your knowledge of the art of government!
And, credit me, I glory to behold you
Dispose of great designs, as if you were
A partner, and no subject of my empire.

PULCHERIA
My vigilance, since it hath well succeeded,
I am confident you allow of yet it is not
Approved by all.

THEODOSIUS
Who dares repine at that
Which hath our suffrage?

PULCHERIA
 One that too well knows
The strength of her abilities can better
My weak endeavours.

THEODOSIUS
In this you reflect
Upon my empress?

PULCHERIA
True: for, as she is
The consort of your bed, 'tis fit she share in
Your cares and absolute power.

THEODOSIUS
You touch a string
That sounds but harshly to me; and I must
In a brother's love, advise you, that hereafter
You would forbear to move it: since she is
In her pure self a harmony of such sweetness,
I Composed of duty, chaste desires, her beauty
(Though it might tempt a hermit from his beads
The least of her endowments. I am sorry
Her holding the first place, since that the second
Is proper to yourself, calls on your envy.
She err! it is impossible in a thought;
And much more speak or do what may offend me.
In other things I would believe you, sister;

But, though the tongues of saints and angels tax'd her,
Of any imperfection, I should be
Incredulous.

PULCHERIA
She is yet a woman, sir.

THEODOSIUS
The abstract of what's excellent in the sex,
But to their mulcts and frailties a mere stranger;
I'll die in this belief.

[Enter **CLEON** with the apple.

CLEON
Your humblest sen-ant,
The lord Paulinus, as a witness of
His zeal and duty to your majesty,
Presents vou with this jewel.

THEODOSIUS
Ha!

CLEON
It is
Preferr'd by him

THEODOSIUS
Above his honour?

CLEON
No, sir;
I would have said his patrimony.

THEODOSIUS
'Tis the same.

CLEON
And he entreats, since lameness may excuse

His not presenting it himself, from me
(Though far unworthy to supply his place)
You would vouchsafe' to accept it.

THEODOSIUS
Further off,

You've told your tale. Stay you for a reward?

Take that.

[Strikes him.

PULCHERIA
How's this?

CHRYSAPIUS
I never saw him moved thus.

THEODOSIUS
We must not part so, sir: a guard upon him!

[Enter **GUARD**.

May I not vent my sorrows in the air,
Without discovery? Forbear the room!

[Exeunt **PULCHERIA**, **CHRYSAPIUS**, **TIMANTUS**, **GRATIANUS** and **GUARD** with **CLEON**.

Yet be within call What an earthquake I feel in me!
And on the sudden my whole fabric totters.
My blood within me turns, and through my veins,
Parting with natural redness, I discern it
Changed to a fatal yellow. What an army
Of hellish furies, in the horrid shapes
Of doubts and fears, charge on me! rise to my rescue,
Thou stout maintainer of a chaste wife's honour,
The confidence of her virtues; be not shaken
With the wind of vain surmises, much less suffer
The devil Jealousy to whisper to me
My curious observation of that
I must no more remember. Will't not be?
Thou uninvited guest, ill-manner 'd monster,
I charge thee, leave me! wilt thou force me to
Give fuel to that fire I would put out?
The goodness of my memory proves my mischief,
And I would sell my empire, could it pur- chase
The dull art of forgetfulness. Who waits there?

[Re-enter **TIMANTUS**.

TIMANTUS
Most sacred sir

THEODOSIUS
Sacred, as 'tis accurs'd,
Is proper to me. Sirrah, upon your life,

To thy insatiate lust, but what was sent
As a dear favour from me? How have I sinn'd
In my dotage on this creature! but to her,
I have lived as I was born, a perfect virgin:
Nay, more, I thought it not enough to be
True to her bed, but that I must feed high,
To strengthen my abilities to cloy
Her ravenous appetite, little suspecting
She would desire a change.

EUDOCIA
I never did, sir.

THEODOSIUS
Be dumb; I will not waste my breath in taxing
Thy base ingratitude. How I have raised thee
Will by the world be, to thy shame, spoke often:
But for that ribald, who held in my empire
The next place to myself, so bound unto me
By all the ties of duty and allegiance,
He shall pay dear for't, and feel what it is,
In a Wrong of such high consequence, to pull down
His lord's slow anger on him! Philanax,
He's troubled with the gout, let him be cured
With a violent death, and in the other world
Thank his physician.

PHILANAX
His cause unheard, sir?

PULCHERIA
Take heed of rashness.

THEODOSIUS
Is what I command
To be disputed?

PHILANAX
Your will shall be done, sir:
But that I am the instrument

THEODOSIUS
Do you murmur?

[Exit **PHILANAX**, with **GUARD**.

What couldst thou say, if that my license should
Give liberty to thy tongue?

[**EUDOCIA** kneeling, points to **THEODOSIUS'** sword.

EUDOCIA
Thou wouldst die? I am not
So to be reconciled. See me no more:
The sting of conscience ever gnawing on thee,
A long life be thy punishment!

[Exit.

FLACCILLA
O sweet lady,
How I could weep for her!
A read. Speak, dear madam, speak.
Your tongue, as you are a woman, while you live
Should be ever moving, at the least, the last part
That stirs about you.

PULCHERIA
Though I should, sad lady,
In policy rejoice, you, as a rival
Of my greatness, are removed, compassion,
Since I believe you innocent, commands me
To mourn your fortune; credit me, I will urge
All arguments I can allege that may
Appease the emperor's fury.

ARCADIA
I will grow too,
Upon my knees, unless he-bid me rise,
And swear he will forgive you.

FLACCILLA
And repent too:
All this pother for an apple!

[Exeunt **PULCHERIA, ARCADIA, FLACCILLA**.

CHRYSAPIUS
Hope, dear madam,
And yield not to despair; I am still your servant,
And never will forsake you, though awhile
You leave the court and city, and give way
To the violent passions of the emperor.
Repentance, in his want of you, will soon find him:
In the mean time, I'll dispose of you, and omit
No opportunity that may invite him

To see his error.

EUDOCIA
Oh!

[Wringing her hands.

CHRYSAPIUS
Forbear, for heaven's sake.

[Exeunt.

SCENE I. A Room in Paulinus' House

Enter **PHILANAX, PAULINUS, GUARD,** and **EXECUTIONERS.**

PAULINUS
This is most barbarous! how have you lost
All feeling of humanity, as honour,
In your consent alone to have me used thus?
But to be, as you are, a looker on,
Nay, more, a principal actor in't, (the softness
Of your former life consider'd,) almost turns me
Into a senseless statue.

PHILANAX
Would, long since,
Death, by some other means, had made you one,
That you might be less sensible of what
You have, or are to suffer!

PAULINUS
Am to suffer!
Let such, whose happiness and heaven depend
Upon their present being, fear to part with
A fort they cannot long hold; mine to me is
A charge that I am weary of, all defences
By pain and sickness batter'd: yet take heed,
Take heed, lord Philanax, that, for private spleen,
Or any false-conceived grudge against me,
(Since in one thought of wrong to you I am
Sincerely innocent,) you do not that
My royal master must in justice punish,
If you pass to your own heart thorough mine;

The murder, as it will come out, discover'd.

PHILANAX
I murder you, my lord! heaven witness for me,
With the restoring of your health, I wish you
Long life and happiness: for myself, I am
Compell'd to put in execution that
Which I would fly from; 'tis the emperor,
The high incensed emperor's will, commands
What I must see perform'd.

PAULINUS
The emperor!
Goodness and innocence guard me! wheels nor racks
Can force into my memory the remembrance
Of the least shadow of offence, with which
I ever did provoke him. Though beloved,
(And yet the people's love is short and fatal,)
I never courted popular applause,
Feasted the men of action, or labour'd
By prodigal gifts to draw the needy soldier,
The tribunes, or centurions to a faction,
Of which I would raise up the head against him.
I hold no place of strength, fortress, or castle,
In my command, that can give sanctuary
To malcontents, or countenance rebellion,
I have built no palaces to face the court,
Nor do my followers' braveries shame his train;
And though I cannot blame my fate for want,
My competent means of life deserve no envy;
In what, then, am I dangerous?

PHILANAX
His displeasure
Reflects on none of those particulars
Which you have mention 'd, though some jealous princes
In a subject cannot brook them.

PAULINUS
None of these!
In what, then, am I worthy his suspicion?
But it may, nay it must be, some informer,
To whom my innocence appear'd a crime,
Hath poison'd his late good opinion of me.
'Tis not to die, but, in the censure of
So good a master, guilty, that afflicts me.

PHILANAX

There is no remedy.

PAULINUS
No! I have a friend yet,
To whom the state I stand in now deliver'd,
(Could the strictness of your warrant give way to it,)
That, by fair intercession for me, would
So far prevail, that, my defence unheard,
I should not, innocent or guilty suffer
Without a fit distinction.

PHILANAX
These false hopes,
My lord, abuse you. What man, when condemn'd,
Did ever find a friend? or who dares lend
An eye of pity to that star-cross'd subject
On whom his sovereign frowns?

PAULINUS
She that dares plead
For innocence without a fee, the empress,
My great and gracious mistress.

PHILANAX
There's your error.
Her many favours, which you hoped should make you,
Prove your undoing. She, poor lady, is
Banish'd for ever from the emperor's presence,
And his confirm'd suspicion, to his wrong,
That you have been over-familiar with her,
Dooms you to death. I know you understand me.

PAULINUS
Over-familiar!

PHILANAX
In sharing with him
Those sweet and secret pleasures of his bed,
Which can admit no partner.

PAULINUS
And is that
The crime for which I am to die? of all
My numerous sins, was there not one of weight
Enough to sink me, if he borrow 'd not
The colour of a guilt I never saw,
To paint my innocence in a deform'd
And monstrous shape? but that it were profane

To argue heaven of ignorance or injustice,
I now should tax it. Had the stars that reign 'd
At my nativity such cursed influence,
As not alone to make me miserable,
But, in the neighbourhood of her goodness to me,
To force contagion upon a lady,
Whose purer flames were not inferior,
To theirs when they shine brightest! to die for her,
Compared with what she suffers, is a trifle.
By her example warn'd, let all great women
Hereafter throw pride and contempt on such
As truly serve them, since a retribution
In lawful courtesies is now styled lust;
And to be thankful to a servant's merits
Is grown a vice, no virtue.

PHILANAX
These complaints
Are to no purpose: think on the long flight
Your better part must make.

PAULINUS
She is prepared:
Nor can the freeing of an innocent
From the emperor's furious jealousy hinder her.
It shall out, 'tis resolved; but to be whisper'd
To you alone. What a solemn preparation
Is made here to put forth an inch of taper,
In itself almost extinguished! mortal poison!
The hangman's sword! the halter!

PHILANAX
'Tis left to you
To make choice of which you please.

PAULINUS
Any will serve
To take away my gout and life together.
I would not have the emperor imitate
Rome's monster, Nero, in that cruel mercy
He shew'd to Seneca. When you have discharged
What you are trusted with, and I have given you
Reasons beyond all doubt or disputation,
Of the empress' and my innocence; when I am dead,
(Since 'tis my master's pleasure, and high treason
In you not to obey it,) I conjure you,
By the hopes you have of happiness here- after,
Since mine in this world are now parting from me,

That you would win the young man to repentance
Of the wrong done to his chaste wife,
Eudocia.
And if perchance he shed a tear for what
In his rashness he imposed on his true servant,
So it cure him of future jealousy,
'Twill prove a precious balsamum, and find me
When I am in my grave. Now, when you please;
For I am ready.

PHILANAX
His words work strangely on me,
And I would do but I know not what to think on't.

[Exeunt.

SCENE II. A Room in the Palace

Enter **PULCHERIA**, **FLACCILLA**, **ARCADIA**, **TIMANTUS**, **GRATIANUS**, and **CHRYSAPIUS**.

PULCHERIA
Still in his sullen mood? no intermission
Of his melancholy fit?

TIMANTUS
It rather, madam,
Increases, than grows less.

GRATIANUS
In the next room
To his bedchamber we watch'd; for he, by signs,
Gave us to understand he would admit
Nor company nor conference.

PULCHERIA
Did he take
No rest, as you could guess?

CHRYSAPIUS
Not any, madam.
Like a Numidsan lion, by the cunning
Of the desperate huntsman taken in a toil,
And forced into a spacious cage, he walks
About his chamber; we might hear him gnash
His teeth in rage, which open'd, hollow groans
And murmurs issued from his lips, like winds

Imprison 'd in the caverns of the earth
Striving for liberty; and sometimes throwing
His body on his bed, then on the ground,
And with such violence, that we more than fear'd,
And still do, if the tempest of his passions
By your wisdom, be not laid, he will commit
Some outrage on himself.

PULCHERIA
His better angel,
I hope, will stay him from so foul a mischief:
Nor shall my care be wanting.

TIMANTUS
Twice I heard him
Say, False Eudocia, how much art thou
Unworthy of these tears! then sigh'd, and straight
Roar'd out, Paulinust was his gouty age
To bepreferr'd before my strength and youth?
Then groan'd again, so many ways expressing
The afflictions of a tortured soul, that we,
Who wept in vain for what we could not help,
Were sharers in his sufferings.

PULCHERIA
Though your sorrow
Is not to be condemn'd, it takes not from
The burthen of his miseries: we must practise,
With some fresh object, to divert his thoughts
From that they are wholly fix'd on.

CHRYSAPIUS
Could I gain
The freedom of access, I would present him
With this petition. Will your highness please
To look upon it: you will soon find there
What my intents and hopes are.

[Enter **THEODOSIUS**.

GRATIANUS
Ha! 'tis he.

PULCHERIA
Stand close,
And give way to his passions; 'tis not safe
To stop them in their violent course, before
They have spent themselves.

THEODOSIUS
I play the fool, and am
Unequal to myself; delinquents are
To suffer, not the innocent. I have done
Nothing, which will not hold weight in the scale
Of my impartial justice; neither feel I
The worm of conscience upbraiding me
For one black deed of tyranny; wherefore, then,
Should I torment myself? Great Julius would not
Rest satisfied that his wife was free from fact,
But, only for suspicion of a crime,
Sued a divorce; nor was this Roman rigour
Censured as cruel: and still the wise Italian,
That knows the honour of his family
Depends upon the purity of his bed,
For a kiss, nay, wanton look, will plough up mischief,
And sow the seeds of his revenge in blood.
And shall I, to whose power the law's a servant,
That stand accountable to none, for what
My will calls an offence, being compell'd,
And on such grounds, to raise an altar to
My anger; though, I grant, it is cemented
With a loose strumpet and adulterer's gore,
Repent the justice of my fury? No.
I should not: yet still my excess of love,
Fed high in the remembrance of her choice
And sweet embraces, would persuade me that
Connivance or remission of her fault,
Made warrantable by her true submission
For her offence, might be excusable,
Did not the cruelty of my wounded honour,
With an open mouth, deny it.

PULCHERIA
I approve of
Your good intention, and I hope 'twill prosper.
[To **CHRYSAPIUS**.
He now seems calm: let us, upon our knees,
Encompass him. Most royal sir

[They all kneel.

FLACCILLA
Sweet brother

ARCADIA
As you are our sovereign, by the ties of nature

You are bound to be a father in your care
To us poor orphans.

TIMANTUS
Shew compassion, sir,
Unto yourself.

GRATIANUS
The majesty of your fortune
Should fly above the reach of grief.

CHRYSAPIUS
And 'tis
Impair'd, if you yield to it.

THEODOSIUS
Wherefore pay you
This adoration to a sinful creature?
I am flesh and blood, as you are, sensible
Of heat and cold, as much a slave unto
The tyranny of my passions, as the meanest
Of my poor subjects. The proud attributes,
By oil-tongued flattery imposed upon us,
As sacred, glorious, high, invincible,
The deputy of heaven, and in that
Omnipotent, with all false titles else,
'Coin'd to abuse our frailty, though compounded,
And by the breath of sycophants applied,
Cure not the least fit of an ague in us.
We may give poor men riches, confer honours
On undeservers, raise, or ruin such
As are beneath us, and, with this puff 'd up,
Ambition would persuade us to forget
That we are men: but He that sits above us,
And to whom, at our utmost rate, we are
But pageant properties, derides our weakness:
In me, to whom you kneel, 'tis most apparent.
Can I call back yesterday, with all their aids
That bow unto my sceptre? or restore
My mind to that tranquillity and peace
It then enjoy'd? Can I make Eudocia chaste,
Or vile Paulinus honest?

PULCHERIA
If I might
Without offence, deliver my opinion

THEODOSIUS

What would you say?

PULCHERIA
That, on my soul, the empress
Is innocent.

CHRYSAPIUS
The good Paulinus guiltless.

GRATIANUS
And this should yield you comfort.

THEODOSIUS
In being guilty
Of an offence far, far transcending that
They stand condemn'd for! Call you this a comfort?
Suppose it could be true, a corsive rather,
Not to eat our dead flesh, but putrify
What yet is sound. Was murder ever held
A cure for jealousy? or the crying blood
Of innocence, a balm to take away
Her festering anguish? As you do desire
I should not do a justice on myself,
Add to the proofs by which Paulinus fell,
And not take from them; in your charity
Sooner believe that they were false, than I
Unrighteous in my judgment? subjects' lives
Are not their prince's tennis-balls, to be bandied
In sport away: all that I can endure
For them, if they were guilty, is an atom
To the mountain of affliction I pull'd on me,
Should they prove innocent.

CHRYSAPIUS
For your majesty's peace,
I more than hope they were not: the false oath
Ta'en by the empress, and for which she can
Plead no excuse, convicted her, and yields
A sure defence for your suspicion of her.
And yet, to be resolved, since strong doubts are
More grievous, for the most part, than to know
A certain loss

THEODOSIUS
'Tis true, Chrysapius,
Were there a possible means.

CHRYSAPIUS

Tis offer'd to you,
If you please to embrace it. Some few minutes
Make truce with passion, and but read, and follow
What's there projected,

[Delivers him a paper.

You shall find a key
Will make your entrance easy, to discover
Her secret thoughts; and then, as in your wisdom
You shall think fit, you may determine of her;

And rest confirm'd, whether Paulinus died
A villain or a martyr.

THEODOSIUS
It may do,
Nay, sure it must; yet, howsoe'er it fall;
I am most wretched. Which way in my wishes
I should fashion the event, I'm so distracted
I cannot yet resolve of. Follow me;
Though 'in my name all names are comprehended,
I must have witnesses in what degree
I have done wrong, or suffer'd.

PULCHERIA
Hope the best, sir.

[Exeunt.

SCENE III. Another Room in the Same

Enter **EUDIOCIA** in sackcloth, her hair loose.

EUDOCIA [Sings]
Why art thou slow, thou rest of trouble, Death,
To stop a -wretch's breath,
That calls on thee, and offers her sad heart
A prey unto thy dart?
I am nor young nor fair; be, therefore, bold:
Sorrow hath made me old,
Deform d and wrinkled; all that I can crave,
Is, quiet in my grave.
Such as live happy, hold long life a jewel;
But to me thou art cruel.
If thou end not my tedious misery;

And I soon cease to be.
Strike, and strike home, then; pity unto me,
In one short hours delay, is tyranny.
Thus, like a dying swan, to a sad tune
I sing my own dirge; would a requiem follow,
Which in my penitence I despair not of,
(This brittle glass of life already broken
With misery,) the long and quiet sleep
Of death would be most welcome! Yet, before
We end our pilgrimage, 'tis fit that we
Should leave corruption and foul sins behind us.
But with wash'd feet and hands, the heathens dare not
Enter their profane temples; and for me
To hope my passage to eternity
Can be made easy, till I have shook off
The burthen of my sins in free confession,
Aided with sorrow and repentance for them.
Is against reason. 'Tis not laying by
My royal ornaments, or putting on
This garment of humility and contrition,
The throwing dust and ashes on my head,
Long fasts to tame my proud flesh, that can make
Atonement for my soul; that must be humbled,
All outward signs of penitence else are useless.
Chrysapius did assure me he would bring me
A holy man, from whom (having discover'd
My secret crying sins) I might receive
Full absolution and he keeps his word.

[Enter **THEODOSIUS** disguised as a Friar, with **CHRYSAPIUS**.

Welcome, most reverend sir, upon my knees
I entertain you.

THEODOSIUS
Noble sir, forbear
The place; the sacred office that I come for

[Exit **CHRYSAPIUS**.

Commands all privacy. My penitent daughter,
Be careful, as you wish remission from me,
That, in confession of your sins, you hide not
One crime, whose ponderous weight, when you would make
Your flights above the firmament, may sink you.
A foolish modesty in concealing aught,
Is now far worse than impudence to profess
And justify your guilt, be therefore free;

So may the gates of mercy open to you!

EUDOCIA
First then, I ask a pardon, for my being
Ingrateful to heaven's bounty.

THEODOSIUS
A good entrance.

EUDOCIA
Greatness comes from above, and I' raised to it
From a low condition, sinfully forgot
From whence it came; and, looking on myself
In the false glass of flattery, I received it
As a debt due to my beauty, not a gift
Or favour from the emperor.

THEODOSIUS
'Twas not well.

EUDOCIA
Pride waited on unthankfulness; and no more
Remembering the compassion of the princess,
And the means she used to make me what I
Contested with her, and with sore eyes seeing
Her greater light as it dimm'd mine, I practised
To have it quite put out.

THEODOSIUS
A great offence;
But, on repentance, not unpardonable.
Forward.

EUDOCIA
O, father! what I now must utter,
I fear, in the delivery will destroy me,
Before you have absolved me.

THEODOSIUS
Heaven is gracious;
Out with it.

EUDOCIA
Heaven commands us to tell truth,
Yet I, most sinful wretch, forswore myself.

THEODOSIUS
On what occasion?

EUDOCIA

Quite forgetting that
An innocent truth can never stand in need
Of a guilty lie, being on the sudden ask'd
By the emperor, my husband, for an apple
Presented by him, I swore I had eaten it;
When my grieved conscience too well knows
I sent it
To comfort sick Paulinus, being a man
I truly loved and favour'd.

THEODOSIUS

A cold sweat,
Like the juice of hemlock, bathes me.

EUDOCIA

And from this
A furious jealousy getting possession
Of the good emperor's heart, in his rage he doom'd
The innocent lord to die; my perjury
The fatal cause of murder.

THEODOSIUS

Take heed, daughter,
You niggle not with your conscience, and religion,
In styling him an innocent, from your fear
And shame to accuse yourself. The emperor
Had many spies upon you, saw such graces,
Which virtue could not warrant, shower'd upon him;
Glances in public, and more liberal favours
In your private chamber-meetings, making way
For foul adultery; nor could he be
But sensible of the compact pass'd between you,
To the ruin of his honour.

EUDOCIA

Hear me, father;
I look'd for comfort, but, in this, you come
To add to my afflictions.

THEODOSIUS

Cause not you
Your own damnation in concealing that
Which may, in your discovery, find forgiveness.
Open your eyes; set heaven or hell before you;
In the revealing of the truth, you shall
Prepare a palace for your soul to dwell in,

Stored with celestial blessings; whereas, if
You palliate your crime, and dare beyond
Playing with lightning, in concealing it.
Expect a dreadful dungeon fill'd with horror,
And never-ending torments.

EUDOCIA
May they fall
Eternally upon me, and increase,
When that which we call Time hath lost its name!
May lightning cleave the centre of the earth,
And I sink quick, before you have absolv'd me,
Into the bottomless abyss, if ever,
In one unchaste desire, nay in a thought,
I wrong'd the honour of the emperor's bed!
I do deserve, I grant, more than I suffer,
In that my fervour and desire to please him,
In my holy meditations press'd upon me,
And would not be kept out; now to dissemble,
When I shall suddenly be insensible
Of what the world speaks of me, were mere madness:
And, though you are incredulous, I presume,
If, as I kneel now, my eyes swoll'n with tears,
My hands heaved up thus, my stretch'd heart-strings ready
To break asunder, my incensed lord
(His storm of jealousy blown o'er) should. hear me,
He would believe I lied not.

THEODOSIUS
Rise, and see him,

[Discovers himself.

On his knees with joy affirm it.

EUDOCIA
Can this be?

THEODOSIUS
My sisters, and the rest there! All, bear witness,

[Enter **PULCHERIA**, **ARCADIA**, **FLACCILLA**, **CHRYSAPIUS**, **TIMANTUS**, and **PHILANAX**.

In freeing this incomparable lady
From the suspicion of guilt, I do
Accuse myself, and willingly submit
To any penance she in justice shall
Please to impose upon me.

EUDOCIA
Royal sir,
Your ill opinion of me's soon forgiven.

PULCHERIA
But how you can make satisfaction to
The poor Paulinus, he being dead, in reason
You must conclude impossible.

THEODOSIUS
And in that
I am most miserable; the ocean
Of joy, which, in your innocence, flow'd high to me,
Ebbs in the thought of my unjust command,
By which he died. O, Philanax, (as thy name
Interpreted speaks thee,) thou hast ever been
A lover of the king, and thy whole life
Can witness thy obedience to my will,
In putting that in execution which
Was trusted to thee; say but yet this once,
Thou hast not done what rashly I commanded,
And that Paulinus lives, and thy reward
For not performing that which I enjoin'd thee,
Shall centuple whatever yet thy duty
Or merit challenged from me.

PHILANAX
'Tis too late, sir:
He's dead; and, when you know he was unable
To wrong you in the way that you suspected,
You'll wish it had been otherwise.

THEODOSIUS
Unable!

PHILANAX
I am sure he was an eunuch, and might safely
Lie by a virgin's side; at four years made one,
Though, to hold grace with ladies, he conceal'd it.
The circumstances, and the manner how,
You may hear at better leisure.

THEODOSIUS
How, an eunuch!
The more the proofs are that are brought to clear thee,
My best Eudocia, the more my sorrows.

EUDOCIA
That I am innocent?

THEODOSIUS
That I am guilty
Of murder, my Eudocia. I will build
A glorious monument to his memory;
And, for my punishment, live and die upon it,
And never more converse with men.

[Enter **PAULINUS**.

PAULINUS
Live long, sir!
May I do so to serve you! and, if that
I live does not displease you, you owe for it
To this good lord.

THEODOSIUS
Myself, and all that's mine.

PHILANAX
Your pardon is a payment.

THEODOSIUS
I am rapt
With joy beyond myself. Now, my Eudocia,
My jealousy puff' d away thus, in this breath
I scent the natural sweetness.

[Kisses her.

ARCADIA
Sacred sir,
I am happy to behold this, and presume,
Now you are pleased, to move a suit, in which
My sister is join'd with me.

THEODOSIUS [To **PULCHERIA**]
Prithee speak it;
For I have vow'd to hear before I grant:
I thank your good instructions.

ARCADIA
'Tis but this, sir:
We have observed the falling out and in
Between the husband and the wife shews rarely;
Their jars and reconcilements strangely take us.

FLACCILLA

Anger and jealousy that conclude in kisses,
Is a sweet war, in sooth.

ARCADIA

We therefore, brother,
Most humbly beg you would provide us husbands,
That we may taste the pleasure oft.

FLACCILLA

And with speed, sir;
For so your favour's doubled.

THEODOSIUS

Take my word,
I will with all convenience; and not blush
Hereafter to be guided by your counsels:
I will deserve your pardon. Philanax
Shall be remember'd, and magnificent bounties
Fall on Chrysapius; my grace on all.
Let Cleon be deliver'd, and rewarded.
My grace on all, which as I lend to you,
Return your vows to heaven, that it may please,
As it is gracious, to quench in me
All future sparks of burning jealousy.

[Exit

EPILOGUE

We have reason to be doubtful, whether he
On whom (forced to it from necessity)
The maker did confer his emperor s part,
Hath given you satisfaction, in his art
Of action and delivery; 'tis sure truth,
The burthen was too heavy for his youth
To undergo: but, in his will, we know,
He was not wanting, and shall ever owe,
With his, our service, if your favours deign
To give him strength, hereafter to sustain
A greater weight. It is your grace that can
In your allowance of this, write him man
Before his time; which, if you please to do,
You, make the player and the poet too.

This biography was initially written in 1830

Very few materials exist for a life of Massinger beyond the entries of the Parish Register or the College Books, and a few slender intimations scattered here and there in the dedications to his plays. From these scanty sources the following brief memoir is derived.

Our author was born at Salisbury in the year 1584: he was the son of Arthur Massinger, a gentleman in the service of Henry, the second Earl of Pembroke. We must not suppose, from his being thus attached to the family of a nobleman, that the father of our poet was a person of inferior birth and station. In those days the word servant carried with it no sense of degradation. The great lords and officers of the court numbered inferior nobles among their followers. We read, in Cavendish's Life of Wolsey, that "my Lord Percy, the son and heir of the Earl of Northumberland, attended upon and was servitor to the lord-cardinal:" and from the situation which Arthur Massinger held in the household of so high and influential a person as the Earl of Pembroke, we might be justly led to argue rather favourably than unfavourably of his family and his connexions. "There were," says Mr. Gifford, "many considerations which united to render this state of dependance respectable and even honourable. The secretaries, clerks, and assistants, of various departments, were not then, as now, nominated by the government, but left to the choice of the person who held the employment; and as no particular dwelling was officially set apart for their residence, they were entertained in the house of their principal. That communication, too, between noblemen of power and trust, both of a public and private nature, which is now committed to the post, was in those days managed by confidential servants, who were despatched from one to the other, and even to the sovereign;" and, indeed, the father of our poet himself was, we know, in one instance thus employed as the bearer of communications from his patron to Elizabeth. We read in The Sidney Letters, "Mr. Massinger is newly come up from the Earl of Pembroke with letters to the queen for his lordship's leave to be away this St. George's Day." This was an errand which would not have been intrusted to the execution of any inconsiderable person: unimportant as the occasion may appear to us, it would not have been regarded in that light by Elizabeth; for no monarch ever exacted from the nobility, and particularly from her officers of state, a more rigid and scrupulous compliance with stated order than this princess.

With regard to the early youth of Massinger, we possess no information whatever. Mr. Gifford supposes that it might have been passed at Wilton, a seat belonging to the Earl of Pembroke, in the neighbourhood of Salisbury; but this mode of disposing of his early years rests on a very improbable conjecture. It may occasionally have happened that the child of a favourite dependant was admitted as the companion of the younger branches of the patron's family, and allowed to receive his education among them; but this was certainly not an ordinary case; and, like Cavendish, a large majority of the great man's servants and dependants "left wife and children, home and family, rest and quietness, only to serve him."—Massinger was most likely educated at the grammar-school of Salisbury, where many distinguished characters have received the rudiments of their education, among whom the elegant and accomplished Addison is to be numbered. But wherever the first years of our poet's life may have been spent, and whatever may have been the nature of his education, we know that at the age of eighteen (May 14, 1602) he was entered at the university of Oxford, and became a commoner of St. Alban's Hall.

Massinger resided at Oxford about four years, and then abruptly left it, without taking any degree. The cause of this sudden departure is ascribed by Mr. Gifford to the death of his father, from whom his supplies were derived: but Davies relates a very different story, and asserts that the Earl of Pembroke, who had sent him to the university and maintained him there, withdrew the necessary allowance in consequence of his having misapplied the time demanded for severer studies, in the pursuit of a more attractive but less profitable description of literature. Each opinion is equally ungrounded on the basis of any substantial evidence, and rests almost entirely on the imagination of the biographer: what slight authority there is favours the latter supposition, which, perhaps, on the whole, is most consistent with the known circumstances of the case. Anthony Wood, who was born, lived, and died at Oxford; who spent his time in collecting and recording the gossip which circulated in the university respecting the characters and conduct of its more distinguished sons; and whose evidence, however indifferent it may be, is the best that can be obtained upon the subject, confirms the representation of Davies:— "Massinger," says Wood, "gave his mind more to poetry and romance, for about four years or more, than to logic and philosophy, which he ought to have done, as he was patronised to that end." This passage corroborates the account of Davies so far as to intimate that patronage was afforded to our author, and that cause of dissatisfaction was given to the patron; but it goes no farther: it does not even state to whom the poet was indebted for assistance, nor that the misapplication of his academic hours was at all resented by the friend from whom the assistance was received: but still Wood is very probably correct in his information that other than his paternal funds were depended upon for maintaining Massinger at the university; and if such was the case, there can be no question from whose hands they must have proceeded; while the simple fact of his having been totally neglected, from the time of his father's death, by the whole of the Pembroke family, till after the demise of the earl, carries with it a strong suspicion that some offence was committed on the side of the poet, and tenaciously remembered on the side of the peer. Henry, the second Earl of Pembroke, died (1601) the year before Massinger was admitted at Oxford; and William, the third earl, to whom the father of Massinger continued attached during life, is universally and justly considered one of the brightest ornaments of the courts of Elizabeth and James. He was a man of generous and liberal disposition; the distinguished patron of arts and learning; and a lover of poetry, which he himself cultivated with some degree of success. It is not probable—it is impossible—that such a man should have allowed the highly talented son of an old and faithful servant of his family to be checked in his course of study, and abandoned to maintain, through the early years of life, a single-handed contest with adversity, for the want of that pecuniary aid which he could have yielded and never missed, unless some strong and decided cause of displeasure had existed. Had Massinger been merely forced to leave the university, as Mr. Gifford supposes, because the funds necessary to maintain him there had failed with the life of his father, we impute an act of illiberality to the Earl of Pembroke which is inconsistent with the whole tenor of his life and character. From whatever source the expenses of our author's education were originally defrayed, their suddenly ceasing argues in favour of the account intimated by Wood and detailed by Davies. If his father had, during his life, supported him at the university, there must have been some reason for the earl's not continuing that support when the father of Massinger was no more; and perhaps the most honourable supposition for both parties is that which represents the earl as offended by the bent of our author's studies and pursuits. By adopting this view of the case we are saved from the painful necessity of either assuming, on the one hand, that a nobleman distinguished among the most amiable characters of his age allowed a highly gifted and meritorious young man, a natural dependant of his house, to languish in the want of that countenance and protection on which he had an hereditary claim; or, on the other hand, that Massinger had incurred the displeasure of his natural and hereditary patron by the commission of some more crying offence.

Every, even the slightest, surmise of Mr. Gifford is deserving attention and respect; but I cannot admit the supposition by which he would account for the alienation that subsisted between the Earl of Pembroke and our author. That distinguished critic has inferred, from the religious sentiments contained in The Virgin Martyr, that Massinger was a Roman catholic, and for that cause neglected by the protector of his father. But if the intimations scattered through this play and others should be received as sufficient evidence of the faith of Massinger, we must, on similar evidence—the intimations contained in Measure for Measure, for instance—conclude that the religion of Shakspeare was the same; and then we are cast back upon our old difficulty, and have to explain why William Earl of Pembroke, a celebrated patron of literary men, and of dramatists in particular, scorned to yield his notice to the catholic Massinger, while (to use the expression of Heminge and Condell) he "prosequuted" the catholic Shakspeare and "his works with so much favour?" There are many reasons for believing Shakspeare to have been a member of the church of Rome; and the patronage afforded him by the Earl of Pembroke proves, that that nobleman extended his liberality to men of genius without any regard to distinctions of faith; but, on the other hand, we have no just grounds for assuming that Massinger really did hold the same opinions. The only evidence we have upon this point, that afforded by the general tone of his writings, is of a most vague and superficial description. What, in fact, can be inferred from it? We may from such a source derive very satisfactory information respecting the sentiments which would be favourably received by the audience, but very little respecting those of the author. The truth is, that though the national religion was reformed in its liturgy and articles, the feelings, prejudices, and superstitions of the people were still almost entirely catholic; and Massinger, like any other dramatic author, writing for the amusement of the people, necessarily addressed them in a language they would understand, and with sentiments that accorded with their own. Besides, as a poet, he would never carry his theological distinctions to his literary labours: Voltaire himself is catholic in his tragedies; and Massinger naturally adopted the creed which was most suitable to the purposes of poetry, and afforded the most picturesque ceremonies and romantic situations. I feel inclined, therefore, to dismiss entirely the theory suggested by Mr. Gifford, for these two reasons; first, supposing our author to have been a catholic, we have no reason for condemning the Earl of Pembroke as a bigot and a persecutor, who would close his eyes to the merits of so great an author, because his faith did not tally with his own; and, secondly, we have no sufficient grounds for supposing him to have been a catholic at all. But with regard to all such visionary conjectures, thinking is literally a waste of thought.

Whatever may have been the nature of Massinger's studies at Oxford, it is quite certain, from the general character of his works, that his time could not have been wasted there; and his literary acquirements, at the period of his leaving the university, appear to have been multifarious and extensive. He was about two-and-twenty (1606) when he arrived in London, where, as he more than once observes, he was driven by his necessities, and somewhat inclined, perhaps, by the peculiar bent of his talents, to dedicate himself to the service of the stage.

The theatre, when Massinger first took up his abode in the metropolis, must have presented attractions of all others the most calculated to excite the interest, and inspire the imagination, of a young man of sensibility, taste, and education like our poet. No art ever attained a more rapid maturity than the dramatic art in England. The people had, indeed, been long accustomed to a species of exhibition, called MIRACLES or MYSTERIES, founded on sacred subjects, and performed by the ministers of religion themselves, on the holy festivals, in or near the churches, and designed to instruct the ignorant in the leading facts of sacred history. From the occasional introduction of allegorical characters, such as Faith, Death, Hope, or Sin, into these religious dramas, representations of another kind, called MORALITIES, had by degrees arisen, of which the plots were more artificial, regular, and connected, and which were entirely formed of such personifications: but the first rough draught of a regular tragedy and comedy—Lord Sackville's Gorboduc, and Still's Gammer Gurton's Needle—were not produced till within the latter half of the sixteenth century, and little more than twenty years before the stage acquired its highest splendour in the productions of Shakspeare.

About the end of the sixteenth century, the attention of the public began to be more generally directed to the drama; and it throve most admirably beneath the cheering beams of popular favour. The theatrical performances which in the early part of Elizabeth's reign had been exhibited on temporary stages, erected in such halls or apartments as the actors could procure, or, more generally, in the yards of the larger inns, while the spectators surveyed them from the surrounding windows and galleries, began to find more convenient and permanent habitations. About the year 1569, a regular playhouse, under the appropriate name of The Theatre, was erected. It is supposed to have stood somewhere in Blackfriars; and, three years after the commencement of this establishment, the queen, yielding to her own inclination for such amusements, and disregarding the remonstrances of the Puritans, granted licence and authority to the servants of the Earl of Leicester ("for the recreation of her loving subjects, as for her own solace and pleasure when she should think good to see them") to exercise their occupation throughout the whole realm of England. From this time the number of theatres increased with the increasing demands of the people. Various noblemen had their respective companies of performers, who were associated as their servants, and acted under their protection; and when Massinger left Oxford, and commenced dramatic author, there were no less than seven principal theatres open in the metropolis.

With respect to the interior arrangements, there were very few points of difference between our modern theatres and those of the days of Massinger. The prices of admission, indeed, were considerably cheaper: to the boxes the entrance was a shilling; to the pit and galleries only sixpence. Sixpence also was the price paid for stools upon the stage; and these seats, as we learn from Decker's Gull's Hornbook, were particularly affected by the wits and critics of the time. The conduct of the audience was less restrained by the sense of public decorum, and smoking tobacco, playing at cards, eating and drinking, were generally prevalent among them. The hours of performance were also earlier: the play commencing at one o'clock. During the representation a flag was unfurled at the top of the theatre; and the stage, according to the universal practice of the age, was strewn with rushes; but, in all other respects, the theatres of Elizabeth and James's days seem to have borne a perfect resemblance to our own. They had their pit, where the inferior class of spectators, the groundlings, vented their clamorous censure or approbation; they had their boxes—rooms as they were called—to which the right of exclusive admission was engaged by the night, for the more affluent portion of the audience; and there were again the galleries, or scaffoldings above the boxes, for those who were content to purchase less commodious situations at a cheaper rate. On the stage, in the same manner, the appointments appear to have been nearly of the same description as at present. The curtain divided the audience from the actors, which, at the third sounding, not indeed of the bell, but of the trumpet, was drawn for the commencement of the performance. Malone, in his account of the ancient theatre, supposes that there were no moveable scenes; that a permanent elevation of about nine feet was raised at the back of the stage, from which, in many of the old plays, part of the dialogue was spoken; and that there was a private box on each side this platform. Such an arrangement would have destroyed all theatrical illusion; and it seems extraordinary that any spectators should desire to fix themselves in a station where they could have seen nothing but the backs and trains of the performers; but, as Malone himself acknowledges the spot to have been inconvenient, and that "it is not very easy to ascertain the precise situation where these boxes really were", it may very reasonably be presumed, that they were not placed in the position that the historian of the English stage has supposed. As to the permanent floor, or upper stage, of which he speaks, he may or may not be correct in his statement. All that his quotations upon the subject really establish is, that in the old, as in the modern theatre, when the actor was to speak from a window, or balcony, or the walls of a fortress, the requisite ingenuity was not wanting to contrive a representation of the place. But with regard to the use of painted moveable scenery, it is not possible, from the very circumstances of the case, to believe him correct in his theory. Such a contrivance could not have escaped our ancestors. All the materials were ready to their hands. They had not to invent for themselves, but merely to adapt an old invention to that peculiar purpose; and at a time when every better-furnished apartment was adorned with tapestry; when even the rooms of the commonest taverns were hung with painted cloths; while all the materials were constantly before their eyes, we can hardly believe our forefathers to have been so deficient in ingenuity, as to have missed the simple contrivance of converting the common ornaments of their walls into the decorations of their theatres. But, in fact, the use of scenery was almost co-existent with the introduction of dramatic representations in this country. In the Chester Mysteries (1268), the most ancient and complete collection of the kind which we possess, is found the following stage direction: "Then Noe shall go into the arke with all his familye, his wife excepte. The arke must be boarded round about; and upon the boardes all the beastes and fowles, hereafter rehearsed, must be painted, that their wordes may agree with their pictures." In this passage we have a clear reference to a painted scene. It is not likely that, in the lapse of three centuries, while all other arts were in a state of rapid improvement, and the art of dramatic writing, perhaps, more rapidly and successfully improved than any other, the art of theatrical decoration should have alone stood still. It is not improbable that their scenes were few; and that they were varied, as occasion might require, by the introduction of different pieces of stage furniture. Mr. Gifford, who adheres to the opinions of Malone, says, "A table with a pen and ink thrust in, signified that the stage was a counting-house; if these were withdrawn and two stools put in their place, it was then a tavern." And this might be perfectly satisfactory as long as the business of the play was supposed to be passing within doors; but when it was removed to the open air, such meagre devices would no longer be sufficient to guide the imagination of the audience, and some new method must have been adopted to indicate the place of action. After giving the subject very considerable attention, I cannot help thinking that Steevens was right in rejecting Malone's theory, and concluding that the spectators were, as at the present day, assisted in following the progress of the story by means of painted moveable scenery. This opinion is confirmed by the ancient stage directions. In the folio Shakspeare, 1623, we read "Enter Brutus in his orchard; Enter Timon in the woods; Enter Timon from the cave." In Coriolanus, "Marcius follows them to the gates and is shut in." Innumerable instances of the same kind might be cited to prove that the ancient stage was not so defective in the necessary decorations as some antiquaries of great authority would represent. "It may be added," says Steevens, "that the dialogue of our old dramatists has such perpetual reference to objects supposed visible to the audience, that the want of scenery could not have failed to render many of the descriptions absurd. Banquo examines the outside of Inverness castle with such minuteness, that he distinguishes even the nests which the martens had built under the projecting part of its roof. Romeo, standing in a garden, points to the tops of fruit-trees gilded by the moon. The prologue speaker to the second part of Henry the Fourth expressly shows the spectators 'This worm-eaten hold of ragged stone,' in which Northumberland was lodged. Iachimo takes the most exact inventory of every article in Imogen's bed-chamber, from the silk and silver of which her tapestry was wrought, down to the Cupids that support her andirons. Had not the inside of the apartment, with its proper furniture, been represented, how ridiculous must the action of Iachimo have appeared! He must have stood looking out of the room for the particulars supposed to be visible within it." The works of Massinger would afford innumerable instances of a similar kind to vindicate the opinion which Steevens has asserted on the testimony of Shakspeare alone. But on this subject there is one passage which appears to me quite conclusive. Must not all the humour of the mock play in The Midsummer Night's Dream have been entirely lost, unless the audience before whom it was performed were accustomed to all the embellishments requisite to give effect to a dramatic representation, and could consequently estimate the absurdity of those shallow contrivances and mean substitutes for scenery devised by the ignorance of the clowns?

In only one respect do I perceive any material difference between the mode of representation at the time of Massinger and at present: in his day, the female parts were performed by boys. This custom, which must in many cases have materially injured the illusion of the scene, was in others of considerable advantage: it furnished the stage with a succession of youths, regularly educated for the art, to fill, in every department of the drama, the characters suited to their age. When the lad had become too tall for Juliet, he had acquired the skill, and was most admirably fitted, both in age and appearance, for performing the part which Garrick considered the most difficult on the stage, because it needed "an old head upon young shoulders," the ardent and arduous character of Romeo. When the voice had "the mannish crack," that rendered the youth unfit to appear as the representative of the gentle Imogen, the stage possessed in him the very person that was wanting to do justice to the princely sentiments of Arviragus or Guiderius.

Such was the state of the stage when Massinger arrived in the metropolis, and dedicated his talents to its service. He joined a splendid fraternity, for Shakspeare, Jonson, Beaumont, Fletcher, Shirley, were then flourishing at the height of their reputation, and the full vigour of their genius. Massinger came among them no unworthy competitor for such honours and emoluments as the theatre could afford. Of the honours, indeed, he seems to have reaped a very fair and equitable portion; of the emoluments, the harvest was less abundant. In those days, very little pecuniary reward was to be gained by the dramatic poet, unless, as indeed was most frequently the case, he added the profession of the actor to that of the author, and recited the verses which he wrote. The distinguished performers of that time, Alleyn, Burbage, Heminge, Condell, Shakspeare, all appear to have died in independent, if not affluent, circumstances; but the remuneration obtained by the poet was most miserably curtailed. The price given at the theatre for a new play fluctuated between ten and twenty pounds; the copyright, if the piece was printed, might produce from six to ten pounds more; in addition to these sums, the dedication-fee may be reckoned, the usual amount of which was forty shillings. Our author appears to have produced about two or three plays every year. Most of them were successful; but, even with this industry and good fortune, his annual income would rarely have exceeded fifty pounds: and we cannot, therefore, feel surprised at finding him continually speaking of his necessities; or that the only existing document connected with his life should be one that represents him in a state of pecuniary embarrassment.

Among the papers of Dulwich College, the indefatigable Mr. Malone discovered the following letter tripartite, which, coming from persons of such deserved celebrity, cannot fail of interesting the reader.

"To our most loving friend, Mr. Phillip Hinchlow, esquire, these.

"Mr. Hinchlow,

"You understand our unfortunate extremitie, and I doe not thincke you so void of Christianitie but that you would throw so much money into the Thames as wee request now of you, rather than endanger so many innocent lives. You know there is xl. more, at least, to be receaved of you for the play. We desire you to lend us vl. of that, which shall be allowed to you; without which, we cannot be bayled, nor I play any more till this be dispatch'd. It will lose you xxl. ere the end of the next weeke, besides the hindrance of the next new play. Pray, sir, consider our cases with humanity, and now give us cause to acknowledge you our true freind in time of neede. Wee have entreated Mr. Davison to deliver this note, as well to witness your love as our promises, and alwayes acknowledgement to be ever

"Your most thankfull and loving friends,
"NAT. FIELD."

"The money shall be abated out of the money remayns for the play of Mr. Fletcher and ours.
"ROB. DABORNE."

"I have ever found you a true loving friend to mee, and in soe small a suite, it beinge honest, I hope you will not fail us.
"PHILIP MASSINGER."

Indorsed.
"Received by mee, Robert Davison, of Mr. Hinchlow, for the use of Mr. Daboerne, Mr. Feeld, Mr. Messenger, the sum of vl.
"ROB. DAVISON."

The occasion of the distress in which these three distinguished persons were involved it is not possible to fathom. We may imagine a thousand emergencies, either creditable or discreditable to the fame of the writers, with which the letter would perfectly tally; but, on such slight and vague intimations, no ingenuity could determine which was most likely to be correct. But from the document a circumstance is ascertained, which, before its discovery, had been called in question. Sir Aston Cockayne, a friend of Massinger, had asserted in a volume of poems, published in 1658, that our author had written in conjunction with Fletcher; Davies doubted this report, but the above letter establishes the fact beyond the possibility of dispute.

Massinger is known to have produced thirty-seven plays for the stage, a list of which is given at the conclusion of this memoir. Sixteen entire plays and the fragment of another, The Parliament of Love, alone are extant. No less than eleven of his productions, in manuscript, were in possession of Mr. Warburton (Somerset Herald), and destroyed with the rest of that gentleman's invaluable collection by his cook, who, ignorant of their worth, used them as waste paper for the purposes of the kitchen.

The great and various merits of the works of Massinger will be better seen in the following volumes than in any elaborate, critical dissertation. If our author be compared with the other dramatic writers of his age, we cannot long hesitate where to place him. More natural in his characters and more poetical in his diction than Jonson or Cartwright, more elevated and nervous than Fletcher, the only writers who can be supposed to contest his pre-eminence, Massinger ranks immediately under Shakspeare himself. Our poet excels, perhaps, more in the description than in the expression of passion; this may in some measure be ascribed to his attention to the fable: while his scenes are managed with consummate skill, the lighter shades of character and sentiment are lost in the tendency of each part to the catastrophe. The melody, force, and variety of his versification are always remarkable. The prevailing beauties of his productions are dignity and elegance; their predominant fault is want of passion.

Massinger's last play—which is unfortunately lost—The Anchoress of Pausilippo, was acted Jan. 26, 1640, about six weeks before his death, which happened on the 17th of March, 1640. He went to bed in good health, says Langbaine, and was found dead in the morning, in his own house on the Bankside. He was buried in the churchyard of St. Saviour's, and the comedians paid the last sad duty to his name, by attending him to the grave.

It does not appear, though every stone and every fragment of a stone has been carefully examined, that any monument or inscription of any kind marked the place where his dust was deposited. "The memorial of his mortality," says Gifford, "is given with a pathetic brevity, which accords but too well with the obscure and humble passages of his life: March 20, 1639-40, buried Philip Massinger, A STRANGER."

Such is all the information that remains to us of this distinguished poet. But though we are ignorant of every circumstance respecting him but that he lived, wrote, and died, we may yet form some idea of his personal character from the recommendatory poems prefixed to his several plays, in which, as Mr. Gifford justly observes, the language of his panegyrists, though warm, expresses an attachment apparently derived not so much from his talents as his virtues: he is their beloved, much-esteemed, dear, worthy, deserving, honoured, long-known, and long-loved friend. All the writers of his life represent him as a man of singular modesty, gentleness, candour, and affability; nor does it appear that he ever made or found an enemy.

PHILIP MASSINGER – A CONCISE BIBLIOGRAPHY

As would be expected many works from this time no longer exist either in part or their entirety. Further many playwrights collaborated on plays or revised them for later performances and we have used the latest position known on each of them for the bibliography below.

Solo Plays
The Maid of Honour, tragicomedy (c. 1621; printed 1632)
The Duke of Milan, tragedy (c. 1621–3; printed 1623, 1638)
The Unnatural Combat, tragedy (c. 1621–6; printed 1639)
The Bondman, tragicomedy (licensed 3 December 1623; printed 1624)
The Renegado, tragicomedy (licensed 17 April 1624; printed 1630)
The Parliament of Love, comedy (licensed 3 November 1624; MS)
A New Way to Pay Old Debts, comedy (c. 1625; printed 1632)
The Roman Actor, tragedy (licensed 11 October 1626; printed 1629)
The Great Duke of Florence, tragicomedy (licensed 5 July 1627; printed 1636)
The Picture, tragicomedy (licensed 8 June 1629; printed 1630)
The Emperor of the East, tragicomedy (licensed 11 March 1631; printed 1632)
Believe as You List, tragedy (rejected by the censor in January, but licensed 6 May 1631; MS)
The City Madam, comedy (licensed 25 May 1632; printed 1658)
The Guardian, comedy (licensed 31 October 1633; printed 1655)
The Bashful Lover, tragicomedy (licensed 9 May 1636; printed 1655)

Collaborations with John Fletcher
Sir John van Olden Barnavelt, tragedy (August 1619; MS)
The Little French Lawyer, comedy (c. 1619–23; printed 1647)
A Very Woman, tragicomedy (c. 1619–22; licensed 6 June 1634; printed 1655)
The Custom of the Country, comedy (c. 1619–23; printed 1647)

The Double Marriage, tragedy (c. 1619–23; Printed 1647)
The False One, history (c. 1619–23; printed 1647)
The Prophetess, tragicomedy (licensed 14 May 1622; printed 1647)
The Sea Voyage, comedy (licensed 22 June 1622; printed 1647)
The Spanish Curate, comedy (licensed 24 October 1622; printed 1647)
The Lovers' Progress or The Wandering Lovers, tragicomedy (licensed Dec 1623; rev 1634; printed 1647)
The Elder Brother, comedy (c. 1625; printed 1637).

Collaborations with John Fletcher and Francis Beaumont
Thierry and Theodoret, tragedy (c. 1607; printed 1621)
The Coxcomb, comedy (1608–10; printed 1647)
Beggars' Bush, comedy (c. 1612–15; revised 1622; printed 1647)
Love's Cure, comedy (c. 1612–15; revised 1625; printed 1647).

Collaborations with John Fletcher and Nathan Field
The Honest Man's Fortune, tragicomedy (1613; printed 1647)
The Queen of Corinth, tragicomedy (c. 1616–18; printed 1647)
The Knight of Malta, tragicomedy (c. 1619; printed 1647).

Collaborations with Nathan Field
The Fatal Dowry, tragedy (c. 1619, printed 1632); adapted by Nicholas Rowe: The Fair Penitent

Collaborations with John Fletcher, John Ford, and William Rowley, or John Webster
The Fair Maid of the Inn, comedy (licensed 22 January 1626; printed 1647).

Collaborations with John Fletcher, Ben Jonson, and George Chapman
Rollo Duke of Normandy, or The Bloody Brother, tragedy (c. 1616–24; printed 1639).

Collaborations with Thomas Dekker
The Virgin Martyr, tragedy (licensed 6 October 1620; printed 1622).

Collaborations with Thomas Middleton and William Rowley
The Old Law, comedy (c. 1615–18; printed 1656).